Anything to do with children's entertainment is a source of controversy: Children's television programs, musical preferences, and leisure activities are frequent sources of debate. Toys and play are often singled out for attention, particularly war toys, sex-typed toys, and video games with aggressive themes. Are these harmful to children? Are they addictive? Alternatively, can parents facilitate children's learning with educational toys?

Toys, Play, and Child Development explores these and other questions. Parental attitudes toward and reactions to war toys are described, as are the children's views themselves. Toys and play are shown to contribute to the development of language, imagination, and intellectual achievement and to be effective in child psychotherapy.

Toys, play, and child development

TOYS, PLAY, AND CHILD DEVELOPMENT

Edited by

Jeffrey H. Goldstein
University of Utrecht,
The Netherlands

CAMBRIDGE
UNIVERSITY PRESS

Published by the Press Syndicate of the University of Cambridge
The Pitt Building, Trumpington Street, Cambridge CB2 1RP
40 West 20th Street, New York, NY 10011-4211, USA
10 Stamford Road, Oakleigh, Melbourne 3166, Australia

© Cambridge University Press 1994

First published 1994

Printed in the United States of America

Library of Congress Cataloging-in-Publication Data
Toys, play, and child development / edited by Jeffrey H. Goldstein.
p.   cm.
Includes bibliographical references and indexes.
ISBN 0-521-45062-4 (U.S. : hard). – ISBN 0-521-45564-2 (U.S. :
  pbk.)
1. Play.   2. Toys – Social aspects.   3. Child development.
I. Goldstein, Jeffrey H.
HQ782.T79   1994
155.4'18 – dc20   93-48514
                                                                 CIP

A catalog record for this book is available from the British Library.

ISBN 0-521-45062-4 hardback
ISBN 0-521-45564-2 paperback

Contents

Acknowledgments

Throughout this project I have had the unwavering support and encouragement of David Hawtin and the British Toy and Hobby Association, to whom I am most grateful. I do not know where I would be without them.

Gill Gray, Brigitte Bach, and Mary Caldecott-Smith of GCI, London, happily, or so it seemed to all concerned, took care of every detail to ensure the smooth flow of the play seminar and the timely delivery of the manuscript.

I thank Maria Bartels, holistic language teacher, for so ably translating some of the material for this book.

Julia Hough, our editor, and Karen Akins, editorial assistant, at Cambridge University Press shared our enthusiasm for this project from the beginning.

With so capable and dedicated a team behind this book, any errors or omissions that remain must be my responsibility.

J.H.G.

Contributors

Birgitta Almqvist
Department of Education
Uppsala University
Box 2109
S–750 02 Uppsala, Sweden

Jeffrey H. Goldstein
Departments of Social &
Organizational Psychology and
Mass Communication & Public
Relations
University of Utrecht
P.O. Box 80140
3508 TC Utrecht, The Netherlands

Ithel Jones
Institute for Behavioral Research
Barrow Hall
University of Georgia
Athens, GA 30602

Anthony D. Pellegrini
Institute for Behavioral Research
Barrow Hall
University of Georgia
Athens, GA 30602

Dorothy G. Singer
Television Research Project
Yale University
New Haven, CT 06520

Jerome L. Singer
Department of Psychology
Yale University
New Haven, CT 06520

Peter K. Smith
Department of Psychology
University of Sheffield
Sheffield S10 2TN, England

Brian Sutton-Smith
Graduate School of Education
University of Pennsylvania
3700 Walnut Street
Philadelphia, PA 19104

Gisela Wegener-Spöhring
Department of General Pedagogics
Waldweg 26
Georg-August University of
Göttingen
3400 Göttingen, Germany

Introduction

JEFFREY H. GOLDSTEIN

This book has its origin in a conversation with D. L. Hawtin, Director General of the British Toy and Hobby Association. He felt that there was little appreciation of why children play, what they learn through play, and how toys can facilitate play and broaden its consequences. There is much research on the subject, I said, and suggested that we invite some leading researchers to discuss their work with an eclectic audience of students, teachers, journalists, people in the toy industry, and others who care for children. Accordingly, with sponsorship from the British Toy and Hobby Association, a seminar was held in London in October 1992. Most of the chapters in this book began as papers for that seminar. To round out these papers, additional chapters were commissioned on subjects, such as sex differences in play, that the crowded seminar agenda did not permit.

Each contributor to this book is a highly regarded expert and researcher in the field of children's play. Furthermore, each has written for nonspecialist audiences of parents, students, and teachers, the audience for this book. These psychologists are not only able researchers, they are individuals sensitive to what children tell us through play. They do not merely speak of children in the abstract, as research subjects, but of children whom we know and were.

Although they share skills and interests, the authors do not always agree among themselves. There are differences in the way they view war play, for example, and in the extent to which play can or should be guided by adults. Certainly in the use of play in child psychotherapy, the therapist must encourage particular forms of play. It should come as no surprise that there is disagreement over these issues. For one thing, there is little or no research on some of these matters. In some cases, there is evidence on different sides of the same question. Furthermore, some of these questions are unlikely to be decided on the basis of empirical evidence alone, but depend also on one's own principles. For instance, some parents will not buy war toys for their children, regardless of whether there is evidence of harm.

Some themes recur throughout the book:

1. Individual differences between children – their sex, degree of imagination and fantasy, motives for play – influence the type and effects of play and their use of toys.
2. A toy itself may influence the nature of play, but children's different styles of play also influence how toys are used. In the relations between toys, play, and child development, each influences the others.
3. There are behavioral, cognitive, aesthetic, and ethical components of play, toys, and video games. Children's play, as well as some toys and video games, can be unaesthetic, violating all sorts of social norms. Play turns the world upside down. According to at least one author (P. K. Smith), toy manufacturers have a moral obligation to draw the line at offensive items, even if harmful effects are unproven.
4. Play does not occur in a vacuum. Important events and relationships in children's lives are reflected in their play themes. Play is also a mirror of social life, but always a distorting mirror, such as one finds in a fun house (which, in a manner of speaking, is what we are talking about). So children enact the gender roles they see around them, as well as the roles of parents, nurses, teachers, and soldiers. If these did not matter to adults, they would not matter to children.

Jerome L. Singer begins with the development of the child's capacity for fantasy and imaginative play. He shows that make-believe play is more than just an enjoyable form of self-entertainment. Imaginative play lays the foundation for a fundamental human capacity of lifelong value – the capacity for thinking about the possible, for wondering "Might this be?" The ability to transform objects or settings into possible alternatives is crucial for adult thought, planning, and creativity.

Early opportunities for make-believe play may be critical. Parental encouragement, reading, and the availability of toys that stimulate imaginative play may be crucial in facilitating imaginative thought. Very young children need more structured or realistic toys that represent common objects in the home – dolls, furnishing, vehicles – in order to engage in pretend play. As their thinking develops, they are able to use less realistic objects in play – blocks, clay, pipe cleaners.

As language increases and they are able to communicate more fully about their pretend activities, children's dependence on realistic objects decreases. This theme is taken up by Anthony Pellegrini and Ithel Jones, who summarize research on toys, play, and language. They demonstrate that toys do not have unidirectional effects on preschool children. The type of language used in play varies with the type of toy (e.g., whether it is a realistic toy) and with the social setting (e.g., whether the child plays alone or with others of the same or the opposite sex). The fact that the same toy is used in different ways is reiterated by Almqvist.

Birgitta Almqvist raises interesting questions about the distinction between educational toys and the rest. By implication, some toys must be noneducational. The notion of an educational toy assumes that the toy awakens the same reactions in every child. This conclusion is false, she believes. The child's own imagination, gender, and age are more crucial factors in play and development than specific toys or play materials. This theme is also found in chapter 6. Almqvist offers suggestions for using ordinary toys to teach specific skills and to stimulate cognitive development.

Two chapters examine aggressive play and war toys. Peter K.

Smith reviews the debate over war toys (guns, action figures, superheroes). Parents and educators of young children disagree about the effects of war toys on children's behavior and development. One view is that such forms of play impoverish the child's imagination and encourage aggressive behavior. Many nurseries and infant schools ban war toys and overt forms of war play. Carlsson-Paige and Levin in *The War Play Dilemma* (1987) argue that war play should be turned to more constructive ends. A contrasting viewpoint is that war play is a natural kind of play, clearly pretense, that does no more than reflect aspects of the adult world and help the child come to terms with it. Professor Smith reports a study conducted in Britain and Italy of parents' attitudes toward their children's war play.

Gisela Wegener-Spöhring writes that aggressive, frightening, and unseemly play themes are frequent and normal parts of children's play. Children usually deal with these themes in ways that make them tolerable for all playmates. If adults become involved, their intervention often destroys the delicate play balance. Adults often forget that play is not real, that it is pretend. Children think of their play as free and under their own control. They often perceive adult restriction of their play as a form of violence, says Wegener-Spöhring. Aggressive play does not reproduce reality; no play does that. Aggressive play is simply fun, dynamic, exciting, usually very physical, and is accompanied by laughter, cries, and onomatopoeia.

Differences in the play of boys and girls, and in their different toy preferences, are discussed by Jeffrey Goldstein. Biological and social origins of sex differences in play are considered, with a focus on aggressive play, war toys, and video games.

Renowned play researcher Brian Sutton-Smith reviews twentieth-century trends in children's play. These include:

- Attempts to reduce physical dangers through organized play, parent–child play, and supervised school play.
- Bringing play indoors, away from dangerous streets and play-

grounds. The computer has hastened the movement from street play to home play.
— Growth in solitary play through fantasy toys, video games, and virtual reality toys.

Sutton-Smith considers the question "Are toys tools of learning?"

Play therapy is discussed by researcher, writer, and child psychotherapist Dorothy G. Singer. This specialized form of psychotherapy utilizes toys, games, and arts and crafts materials as vehicles for expression of conflicts, fears, unresolved wishes, and parental or sibling concerns. Through symbolic play, children cast these concerns into miniaturized forms in order to confront the negative effects of anger, distress, sadness, shame, and humiliation. Using two poignant examples from her clinical experience, Dr. Singer illustrates play therapy techniques.

1

Imaginative play and adaptive development

JEROME L. SINGER

In his intriguing account of a possible way in which human consciousness may have evolved, the philosopher Daniel Dennett has written:

> our ancestors, like us, took pleasure in various modes of undirected self-exploration – stimulating oneself over and over again and seeing what happened. Because of the plasticity of the brain, coupled with the innate restlessness and curiosity that lead us to explore every nook and cranny of our environment ...it is not surprising that we hit upon strategies of self-stimulation or self-manipulation that led to the inculcation of habits and dispositions that radically altered the internal communicative structure of our brains, and that these discoveries became part of the culture – memes – that were then made available to all. (Dennett, 1991, p. 209)

I cite this evolutionary notion because I propose that children's play, with its repetitive and exploratory characteristics, represents not only fun but a critically important feature of their development of cognitive and emotional skills. Considering the various forms play takes, it is easy to identify the possible value of sensorimotor games for enhancing physical skills and even of games with rules for modeling early forms of orderly thought or even morality.

The value of pretending and of make-believe play seems less obvious; indeed, many parents are uncomfortable when they watch their toddlers or preschoolers pushing blocks and toy figures around while talking out loud to themselves. I hope to show, however, that what Jean Piaget (1962) called *symbolic play* is not just a passing feature of growth en route to the emergence of logical, orderly thought. Rather, it is an intrinsically adaptive feature of our human condition. Pretend play serves the child well for self-entertainment and for assimilating the complexities of the world. But it is also the foundation of a long-term incorporation and consolidation of a major human characteristic: our human imagination, our capacity through consciousness to form experiences into stories, to manipulate memory representations of our physical and social worlds into new scenarios. We can travel mentally through time and space, and not only entertain ourselves to pass the time but also explore a range of possible futures, of alternative courses of action. We can sustain ourselves in periods of stress with the hope generated by such imagined explorations.

Making sense of one's world as a child

Let me ask you to use your adult imaginations to accompany me in a brief thought experiment and to travel backward in time to the mind of a 2- or 3-year-old child. Lest such exercises seem trivial, let me mention that I recently had the good fortune to participate in another conference here in London that brought together philosophers, behavioral researchers, and neuroscientists discussing for 3 intense days the nature of human consciousness. Our highly respected chair, a philosopher, had once written a very provocative essay on the mind of a bat, attempting to capture what kinds of consciousness could possibly exist in a blind flying rodent that steers its way around by using the echoes of its emitted sounds to guide it. Lest you conclude that this is just whistling in the dark, recall that Nagel's (1974) study has evoked very useful intellectual analysis. But we can do better in imagining childhood consciousness because we all have at least some memories of our own childhoods, and those of us who are parents, teachers, pediatricians, or careful observers of children can also surmise from children's gestures and verbalizations what they may be experiencing.

I do not propose that we can fully recapture our childish minds. The research of Piaget, the analyses of Schachtel (1959), and the whole thrust of modern cognitive psychology suggest that memory is an active process constantly reshaping and restructuring those external events and objects we have formed into mental representations. Perhaps we would have greater success if, as the late Silvan Tomkins once suggested, we placed you as an adult in an oversized crib "clothed only in diapers, surrounded by oversized blocks, looked down upon by a huge face of a giantess mother with a loud, booming...voice emitting sweet nothings...pinched, tweaked, poked, and fondled" (Tomkins, 1970, p. 109). In a situation like this, in which the sizes and sounds and smells were greatly amplified, you as an adult in this context of babyhood might be surprised at how many childhood memories would return. The psychoanalyst's couch puts many adults in a somewhat analogous situation; you as a grown person are lying on a bed, with another adult sitting next to you, a situation that you are unlikely to experience unless you are in a hospital but that is reminiscent of being put to bed as a child. No wonder so many seemingly childhood memories return during those 50-min hours (Singer, 1974).

If I have created a memory-enhancing mood, you can now retrieve some of your own recollections, the look of your bedroom when you were 3 or 4, the strange sounds from the street that we know to be cars and trucks or passing airplanes but that to a child may sound like the frightening roars of monsters. William James (1890/1952) once referred to the child's world as one of "booming, buzzing confusion." We know from recent research that there is more orderliness wired into our brains, so that certain shapes, objects, and spatial relationships are identified very early by babies and toddlers even without much experience. Nevertheless, there is much that looms large in the physical world and much that seems incomprehensible in the social interactions that surround the child.

What can the poor child do? She can begin to try to deal with a miniature world of downsized objects and people where *she* is the giantess and the trucks, cars, and airplanes are easily manipulable. She can reshape her own bedtime or feeding experience with the help of some props we adults may offer – dolls, toy beds, or toy kitchen tables. She can come to grips with what are often major crises, such as a battle over feeding or messy toileting, but "writing" the scenarios herself and putting dolls into the now miniaturized situations and experiencing the power of watching them suffer as she pretends to be Momma. Freud (1920/1962), drawing on the repetitive play of his 18-month-old grandson, introduced a concept called *repetition-compulsion,* which he reduced in characteristic fashion to the child's efforts to master a fear of maternal abandonment. Not to be outdone, my wife and I recently reported observations of our comparably aged granddaughter, who played repetitively a much more elaborate "airport" game with a few toy props and many sound effects – although we doubt that the child really knew what airplanes or landing fields were (Singer & Singer, 1990). We proposed that this kind of play was broader than just the working out of psychosexual conflicts. Rather, it was an exemplification of the child's fundamental need to make sense of the large, the looming, and the loud in her world by forming manageable units and exploring these strange objects over and over again because they contained so much that was novel to her, if obvious to us (see Table 1.1).

Some benefits of pretend play

Let me summarize briefly the thrust of much of the research and theorizing about cognitive and emotional development carried out in the past few decades as it bears on imaginative play (see Table

Table 1.1. *Stages of play*

Stage I 0–2 years	*Imitation* 1. Use of reflexes 2. Repetition of sounds and movements 3. Beginnings of symbolic imitation
	Practice and mastery 1. Sensory play – tasting, smelling, making sounds 2. Ritualistic play 3. Simple make-believe
Stage II 2–5 years	*Symbolic play* 1. Play that distorts reality; pretend, pure assimilation 2. Implies representation of absent object 3. Parallel play 4. Compensatory play
Stage III 7– years	*Games with rules*[a] 1. Institutional, hide and seek, hopscotch 2. Board games

[a]Games with rules involve competition, codes that are institutionalized, or temporary, spontaneous agreements.

1.2). Making believe seems an inherent human tendency, a major way in which the child explores novelty and, by repetition and restructuring, forms those critical organized mental structures that nowadays are called *schemas* and that form the building blocks of wisdom or efficient memory. In the course of make-believe play the child, who apparently talks out loud most of what we adults call *thought,* hears himself speak and practices new words, enhancing vocabulary. Such play also involves the special form of the representation of one's world that we call *mental imagery* – pictures or sounds in the mind – which have important practical value. No toy train or cowboy looks exactly like the one the child may have seen in a picture book or in real life. Thus, the child begins to use images in a flexible fashion, and this ability to approximate rather than to try to represent reality in a fully accurate, videotapelike fashion opens the way for a major advance in

Table 1.2. *Benefits of play*

  1. Motor skills developed
  2. Senses sharpened
  3. Expression of emotions – empathy
  4. Sharing, turn taking – harmony
  5. Ordering, sequencing
  6. Delay of gratification
  7. Vocabulary growth
  8. Concentration increased
  9. Flexibility
 10. Role taking
 11. Expansion of imagination and creativity

thought that the British psychologist Alan Leslie (1987) has called the *metarepresentational*.

We shall return shortly to that important concept but must next mention that pretend play is related also to the emotional experience of the child. There is increasing evidence that we are biologically endowed, as Darwin long ago surmised (Darwin 1872/1965), with a limited but differentiated set of emotions (Izard, 1991). These emotions are generally evoked by mismatches between our expectations in a given situation and the new information we confront (Mandler, 1984; Singer, 1974; Tomkins, 1962). Our negative emotions such as terror, fear, anger, or sadness are a consequence of the suddenness, and the persistence over time of such incongruity. Our positive emotions follow on how quickly we can match the new information to our well-established store of schemas (joy and laughter) or whether the novelty is moderate enough so that it invites exploration without excessive fear (interest, excitement) (Singer, 1974; Singer & Singer, 1990; Tomkins, 1962). During imaginative play the child, by reducing the features of the external world or of social situations to manageable size, reduces the large incongruities between what he already knows and the massive complexity of the adult world. Thus, with a few toys and blocks, a child can experience the interest and curiosity of moderate novelty and the joy as, through repetition, each element of the game becomes more and more familiar.

With practice in make-believe play, children realize that they have a means of controlling negative emotions; yet, in the story line of the ongoing game they can also express emotions of fear, anger, and distress, and they can experience the excitement of trying new variations and the joy of bringing the play to a familiar conclusion. As children grow and their floor play or talking out loud gives way to the necessity for orderliness in school, they retain the awareness both of the joy of such miniaturizing of their world and of the ways in which it allows emotional expression in a more controlled fashion. Isn't this the basis for the flowering of the private or internal imagination that occurs, at least for some children, during middle childhood and adolescence (Singer & Singer, 1990)?

Although all children show some initial tendency to engage in imaginative play, we find considerable individual differences in the reliance on and richness of such play even by age 3 or 4. Psychologists are now in wide agreement that there are five major trait dimensions of personality. That is, all of us show variable degrees of representing ourselves as (1) Extroverted, (2) Agreeable, (3) Conscientious, (4) Emotionally Stable or Neurotic, and (5) Open or Thoughtful, Curious, and Imaginative (McCrae & John, 1992). Although the research links have yet to be fully forged, I propose that children who early on have practiced and have been encouraged in imaginative play may, as adolescents and adults, be persons who will score high on the measures of the Openness or Thoughtfulness factor. Our research studies of 3- and 4-year-old children followed for 1 year indicate that those who played more often at make-believe or who developed imaginary playmates were also reported by observers to be more likely to smile and laugh during the play school situation, more persistent, more cooperative, and less likely to be angry, aggressive, or sad. In studies of imaginative older children, we find them to be less unwarrantedly aggressive, less impulsive, and better able to discriminate reality from fantasy (Singer & Singer, 1981; Singer & Singer 1990).

Pretend play and the child's theory of mind

Let me now return to the important concept I touched on in passing earlier: the significance of make-believe play for the child's development of a metarepresentational ability, to use Leslie's term. Leslie has carried out various studies and reviewed available literature to suggest that a crucial feature of imaginative play is its linkage to the child's ability to develop a concept of the mind and of different ways of manipulating mentally the representations of objects and situations stored in memory. The British psychologist and philosopher Max Velmans (1990) has argued persuasively that all human experience of the world consists of representations; that is, the human brain, with its peculiar structure and its storage of schemas, projects on the objects of the environment very different features and properties than would be perceived by the bat or even the chimpanzee. These human representations then become the bases for our memories, pains, and anticipations of future situations (Velmans, 1990). Leslie's notion of metarepresentation, as I understand it, suggests that we must in our full maturity also learn that we can manipulate and reshape mentally the ways in which we store memory pictures or sounds of objects and events. We need to deal with fuzzy resemblances, and in this way we can learn to be mentally playful, to develop alternative mental scenarios or fantasies. In imaginative play the child first tries to be fairly literal, but the games would not work if the child needed an *exact* replica of a real truck or a real stove, which, after all, is not available. So the child who plays at pretending is finding out that many things that *sort of* look like others can be manipulated and played with, and eventually learns that many things can be played with in the privacy of the mind.

Not all children grasp this concept. Leslie has proposed that autistic children, who rarely play imaginatively, seem never to be able to make the step toward metarepresentational thought. Studies suggest that even mentally retarded children, who do play make-believe games, are more capable of recognizing the possibility of a mind than are the autistic children who may actually surpass them in IQ (Leslie, 1987). The importance of a child's developing a "theory of mind" has lately become a hot topic among developmental psychologists.

A simple experiment now much used in research demonstrates the developmental process by which the child becomes aware that others may have different beliefs or expectations than oneself. A child observes two boxes, A and B. The experimenter puts a toy under Box A in plain view of this child and another adult. The other adult then leaves the room. The experimenter moves the toy from under Box A to under Box B. "Where is the toy?" she asks the child. The child clearly indicates Box B. Then the other adult returns to the room. "Where will he look for the toy?" asks the experimenter of the child. Generally, children below age 4 will point to Box B, thus failing to separate their own current knowledge from that of another person who cannot have that knowledge. At ages 4 and 5 the children usually have developed a greater sense of the independence of thoughts and of the possibility that one can hold mistaken beliefs (Leslie, 1987; Wellman, 1990). Thus, as Flavell has pointed out in describing Wellman's experiments, for children of 3 "their model of the mind is that of a container that passively copies reality rather than that of a constructive processor that actively – and sometimes inaccurately – interprets or construes it. This 'copy container' model of the mind leads them to expect that beliefs will always mirror reality" (Flavell, 1991, p. 741). Such children below ages 4 or 5 will continue to expect beliefs to copy reality and thus cannot grasp that the adult returning from outside will hold a different belief than they do.

I have gone into some detail here to call attention to the great importance of the child's developing a sense that he or she can manipulate images, memories, and toys into various versions of reality. Given this ability, the metarepresentational style or the awareness of the flexibility of mind, I propose, as does Leslie, that make-believe or pretend play is critical for developing in the child a full-fledged theory of mind, an awareness that one can manipulate toys or imaginary playmates and then gradually transform these into more general ideas. Leslie (1987) has tried to show that in pretend play a child learns to use fuzzy or somewhat vague representations of objects and then to treat them as possibilities. The concept of possibility, the ability to think in the subjunctive mode of "might this be?", is a critical outcome of playing imaginative games, and it clears the way for the child's gradual awareness of the distinction between fantasy and reality (Singer & Singer, 1990). In Figure 1.1, based on two figures in Leslie (1987), we see how simple make-believe can play a role in the child's understanding that representations of real objects can be manipulated for a variety of uses in the privacy of one's own consciousness.

More research is still needed to relate pretend play to awareness of the distinction between one's own mind and another's. I propose, however, that a critical feature of such play is that the child, by manipulating toys that look only partly like real objects, by reshaping the story lines, and by acting the parts of the different characters, is setting a firm foundation for developing the rich imagination that can be adaptive in adult life and is clarifying the distinction between reality and fantasy by learning how to manipulate and move into and out of the play role. The floor make-believe play of a child, if suitably nurtured, can be a critical step for his or her ultimate mental development.

Factors that enhance imaginative play

I have already suggested that to some degree all children, except perhaps those born with the type of brain damage that is reflected in autism, show signs of make-believe play by the beginning of their third year. Yet, we find considerable individual variation in the frequency and complexity of such play among children in the

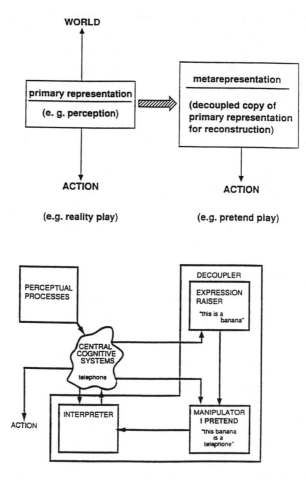

Figure 1.1 Alan Leslie's proposed models for the way the child develops meta-representations in which perceived real objects and their mental images are transformed into a system that allows the child to treat them as possibilities. The upper half depicts the general system, the lower half the specific process by which a perceived object (banana) can be transformed by the child (telephone) for play purposes. (From "Pretense and Representation. The Origins of 'Theory of Mind' " by A. M. Leslie, 1987. Copyright 1987 by the American Psychological Association. Reproduced by permission.)

3- to 5-year period. Our own research and our review of the research of others point to particular features of the child's family situation and general environment that initiate, sustain, and enhance imaginative play (Singer & Singer, 1990). I summarize these briefly and then consider the special role of toys and games in the flowering of the human imagination.

The earliest signs of pretend play emerge between 18 months and 2 years of age. These often take the form of pretending to drink water from an empty cup or, moving to a higher level of transformation, pretending to feed a doll from an empty cup. A further level of transformation involves pretending that a plastic horse is a child who is then fed from an empty bowl or is tucked into a "bed" represented by an empty box (Fein, 1981a, 1987). Although it is often difficult to tell if toddlers would initiate such pretending completely on their own, we do have indications from Fein's observational studies that such play emerges earlier when parents, usually mothers, show active participation, talking to and laughing with the child while themselves carrying out make-believe games. Recently, while we were babysitting with our 27-month-old granddaughter at a park alongside the Connecticut River, she led us to the water's edge and mentioned "fishing." We bent some small branches into a rough fishing pole shape, and she took one and pretended she was fishing by dipping it into the water. This initiated a fairly extended game in which she "caught" a fish and then pretended to take it off the edge of the "pole" and eat it. Our amazement at her precocious make-believe play was mitigated somewhat when, later that day, her mother spontaneously mentioned that she and little Olivia had been "fishing" at that very spot just 2 days before.

However initiated, our own observations and the research literature point to the readiness, indeed the eagerness, of children for some kind of make-believe play between their second and third years. Studies by Diana Shmukler (1981) have shown that parents or other caregivers may initiate make-believe games and then step back and allow the children to play on their own. Such supportive but not overly intrusive guidance may play a critical role in fostering later spontaneous initiation of imaginative play in children. In general, the research literature is consistent in indicating that children whose parents read simple picture books to them or who tell them stories regularly at bedtime are more likely to be scored by objective observers as showing more imaginative play at schools (Singer & Singer, 1990).

Telling and reading stories and initiating make-believe play are certainly important contributions from parents or other adult caregivers. Making play space available where possible or tolerating the children's use of a corner even of one's busy kitchen or parlor may also be important. Parents also enhance children's make-believe play by simply tolerating it. All too often, busy parents are impatient with such games or ignorant parents may fear that the preschool child's overt self-talk reflects "craziness." Scornful put-downs of make-believe or failure to curb older siblings' teasing of a younger child's pretending may lead to a withering of practice of imaginative game skills. There is good evidence that the development of imaginary friends or playmates may be a creative step for many children, often only children or first-borns; such imaginary companions are also associated with other forms of imaginative play (Singer & Singer, 1990). Parents who scorn their 3-year-old's pretend friends or mock the child when asked that a seat at the picnic table be reserved for such friends are unwittingly putting further obstacles in the path of the cognitive and emotional growth of the child. Indeed, research shows that children with imaginary playmates may often be better behaved and, later, more creative (Singer & Singer, 1990).

In effect, then, parents can enhance their child's development of imaginative skills through storytelling, reading, and even floor play with them and also through toleration, indeed enjoyment, of the child's pretend games. There is more they can do to foster imaginative play. They can provide the child (within the limits of their means) appropriate playthings, dress-up clothes, or toys that suggest and sustain imaginative play. Let us turn now to some specific issues that bear on the value, appropriateness, and implications of toys for stimulating the child's imagination.

The special functions of toys

Some of the earliest known toys are play rattles preserved from the ancient Sumerian cultures of the Middle East that date to 2600 B.C. That they may have had a pretend game role is suggested by the fact that they took the form of animals rather than simply functional noisemaker shapes. If we survey the range of toys across time periods and cultures, we find that many of the most popular playthings are unstructured materials made from natural or household materials – shells, bones, sticks, or strings (Singer & Singer, 1990). The bent-branch pretend fishing pole mentioned earlier seemed quite satisfactory for our granddaughter, allowing her to spend a half hour of happy time.

The properties of particular kinds of toys, their realism or structured quality, their mechanical complexity, and their relationship to household or adventurous functions, are all issues that may bear on their value for imaginative play. A very simple toy or object can stimulate a lengthy imaginative game. Mary Ann Pulaski found, for example, that significantly more varied themes and richer fantasy were elicited by the minimally structured materials presented to children from kindergarten through second grade than were elicited by highly structured toys (Pulaski, 1973). Minimally structured toys in her study included drawing paper, paints, Play Doh, wooden blocks, cardboard cartons, pipe cleaners, rag dolls, and costumes. Highly structured toys included plastic molds or cutters for use with Play Doh, a service station, a metal dollhouse, Barbie dolls, a GI Joe doll, and specific outfits for these dolls – a nurse's uniform, a bride's dress, an army uniform, and an astronaut's suit.

In another study, 4- and 5-year-old children, who were observed in small groups as they played, used dress-up materials, a phone, puppets, and stuffed animals more often in social pretend play than such items as puzzles, Legos, small blocks, and coloring materials (Connolly, Doyle & Reznick, 1988). These low-structure items were used more often in a social nonpretend context. Large blocks and a miniature airport and farm were used equally in both contexts. An interesting finding is that nontoy objects such as a wastebasket were used more often in pretend than nonpretend activities, which seems to suggest that children do enjoy using an object in symbolic ways and that, by the ages of 5 to 7, they will carry out transformations more often than younger children (Connolly et al., 1988).

Other studies show that very young children need more structured toys representing commonplace objects in their environment (home furnishings, dolls, vehicles) in order to engage in pretend play. As children's representational skills become more developed, they are able to use less realistic objects in their play (blocks, clay, pipe cleaners, boxes, cardboard tubes) and, consequently, can make more transformations. As their use of language increases and they are able to communicate more about their pretend acts, children's dependence on more realistic objects decreases. Many of the studies focused on middle-class children, who have had greater exposure to all kinds of toys than have poorer children. When they are presented with a wide array of toys in an experimental setting, it is not surprising that children in lower socioeconomic groups initially play more imaginatively with highly structured toys because of their immediate meaningfulness and novelty.

In her study of low-income, predominantly African-American 3½- and 5-year-olds, Vonnie McLoyd found that highly structured toys increased the frequency of noninteractive pretend play among 3½-year olds (McLoyd, 1983). Her results are consistent with our belief that younger children will play more with replicas of everyday objects. The older children in her study engaged in many more substitutions with low-structure objects in their play than did the younger ones, which again is consistent with the idea that pretend play increases with age. The older children, especially the girls, also played more cooperatively than the younger ones, but highly realistic toys did not influence this cooperative play. The types of roles the children enacted were not related to the structure of the toys. Girls, for example, most frequently played familial games, whereas boys preferred fantastic games, a finding similar to our results.

We have seen children play with elaborately constructed toys, motorized toys, wind-up objects, and even Transformer cars for a short while because the familiarity of the toy matches their preestablished schemas and evokes the affect of joy. But these toys often end up at the bottom of the toy chest, their batteries dead. Children choose large blocks, Legos, miniature people, and makeshift objects for longer periods of sustained play. We have also observed that children will initially respond to an opposite-sex-typed toy but then go back to same-sex toys for longer play periods.

Working under the auspices of the Yale Family Television Research Center, Rena Repetti observed slightly older children (aged 5½–7½) in order to explore how their sex stereotyping might be linked to their parents' sex-role attitudes. She found that there was a strong maternal correlation with children's toy stereotypes. The children who chose the more traditionally sex-linked toys were more likely to be those whose parents responded to gender role questionnaires in very traditional ways (Repetti, 1984). Repetti showed pictures of 10 different toys to preschoolers and asked them to indicate whether it was "for boys," "for girls," or "for both boys and girls" to play with. The children were also asked about 16 adult occupations and whether the job was for men, women, or both. Children seemed to be aware of traditional sex stereotypes, assigning planes and jeeps to boys and toy mixers and dolls to girls. The tendency to sex-type toys was significantly related to the child's tendency to stereotype occupations.

The kinds of toys children play with may also determine their uniqueness of response. Brian Sutton-Smith presented kindergartners with male- and female-sex-typed toys and asked them for alternative uses for these toys. Although the children were familiar with both kinds of toys, their play experiences with them had been different. As a result, if the toy was same-sex, the child ascribed more unique responses to it, which suggests that play experiences with the toy contributed to a child's ability to create such responses

(Sutton-Smith, 1968). Another study also sought to examine sex-typed toys and children's ability to suggest new or innovative ways of using them. Such toys were presented to children in Grades 1 to 3 by Erica Rosenfeld (1975). The children were asked to think of strange, exciting, and interesting ways in which they could change the toys so that boys and girls might have more fun playing with them. Both girls and boys presented more varied ideas for improving the masculine toys. It appears that these toys had more potential for unique or creative use.

While there remain many intriguing research questions about the most suitable toys for enhancing imaginative play at different ages or in different settings, we can draw some tentative conclusions based on the literature and our observational studies:

1. Toys that can serve multiple functions seem to have the longest play life and are used more extensively in children's development of story materials. A newspaper cartoon pinned up in our laboratory shows one child calling another to see what's in his room — "It's the best toy ever! It's a fort and a space shuttle, a bus, a pirate ship, a sled, a clubhouse, and a castle. And Mommy was just going to throw it away!" There on the floor is a large empty cardboard parcel post box.

Toys that possess such possibilities and work well from about age 3 through the early school years include various types of construction blocks. These provide opportunities for eye–hand coordination but soon also allow for the building of towns, castles, and space stations, as well as the physical settings for elaborate pretend games of adventure, exploration, or, in general, the miniaturization of the adult world into manageable and entertaining stories.

2. For the very young, easily handled, familiar household object simulations seem suitable, especially those relevant to the daily activities of the child. A small kitchen set can encourage, first, largely repetition of what the child sees. Then gradually the imitation of parents' cooking or serving meals becomes elaborated into fragmentary and then increasingly complex story lines. Recently, one of our grandchildren, just a little over 2, was being

readied to leave her crib for a large bed in anticipation of the advent of a new child. At first she seemed eager, but after a couple of nights in the new bed, she asked for her crib. We purchased a toy bedroom set for her, played with her to set up a story, and then noticed how she followed up on her own, incorporating some other small home toys and dolls into the game of putting children to bed. Within a few days, the crib was packed away and she enjoyed her new bed, where she could scrunch up her "funny pillow" and listen to a bedtime story from one of her parents.

For both younger and older children, clusters of toys like tea sets or restaurant kits may have a sustaining value, first in the solitary make-believe of the 2- or 3-year-old and then in the more complex sociodramatic play of the 4- and 5-year-old. Here, too, dress-up clothes come in handy – simple hand-me-downs from adults or, often, specially manufactured, flexible play clothes that can be used again and again in a variety of stories.

3. Clusters of related toy figures are especially conducive to the development of pretend story lines. These can vary from groups of construction workers, train passengers and engineers, space shuttle astronauts, camera operators, and explorers to toy animals or even dinosaurs, cowboys, pirates with treasure chests, and toy ships. Our observations on gender differences in play suggest that such sets should either include both male and female characters in costumes that cut across traditional sex-role lines or should be androgynous so that boys and girls will use them flexibly.

Other chapters will focus on the special problem of war toys and the mimicry of violence. Here I should like to emphasize the implications of such toy clusters, including toy soldiers, for imaginative play. In research for our recent book on make-believe play (Singer & Singer, 1990), we read scores of autobiographical accounts of childhood play of the famous and near-famous, many of them in Edith Cobb's remarkable collection of childhood reminiscences housed in the library of Teachers College, Columbia University. Toy soldiers were extensively played with and judged as precious toys by men, and some women, who later went on to peaceful literary, scientific, or other creative pursuits.

I myself enjoyed my set of wooden British redcoats provided me at about age 4. They became the basis for many interesting adventure themes in my play over several years. Naturally, as an American boy, I never thought to use them as our adversaries in the Revolutionary War of 1776; only years later did I realize that they were supposed to represent British soldiers. My family maintained strong pacifist values, and I later privately vowed when I went into military service to avoid shooting anyone. Fortunately, despite being in combat in World War II, I never had to fire at a person.

A comparable and more extravagant instance of an American boy early on receiving British soldiers, a Scottish marching band, is described in a charming account entitled "Small-Scale War" in the Talk of the Town section of *The New Yorker* magazine for May 1992 (pp. 30–31). This boy, apparently from a far more affluent family than mine, went on over the next few years to collect dozens of such soldier groups, from dragoons to pirates to gladiators. As he stated to the writer, "since children are children," one day the gladiators and charioteers might play in their original Ben Hur format, but on another day they'd be marshaled as reinforcements for the battle at the Alamo.

What became of this man? Was he stirred by his pretend games to find a career in the military, eventually responsible for mass killings as a general? Not so. He did a stint as a film writer, creating unproduced scripts about military adventure, but finally ended up as a captain of industry. His name is James Delson, and now he may be the world's largest toy-soldier retailer, with more than 2 million play warriors in his Jersey City warehouse and 3,000 regular customers. He, too, claims to be a pacifist.

While I certainly do not wish to propose that providing millions of children with toy soldier sets would alleviate real violence in the world and generate pacifism, I do want to emphasize that such toys can be conducive to generating imaginative play without provoking overtly violent behavior. I am much more concerned about the millions of children who have no toys, no parents who tell stories or read to them, and no sense of history but who do have available *real* guns and who are stimulated to imitation by older peers and by the heavy doses of daily exposure to realistic violence on television. It could be argued that one reason some children act out aggressive behavior directly (in addition to imitating the adult violence they may experience in the family or vicariously) is that they have not had sufficient development of their own narrative and metarepresentational skills early on. That is, they have not practiced, starting with pretend play, their capacity to play out possibilities and situations in a miniaturized mental world, and by so doing learned to explore negative as well as positive consequences of linking direct actions to wishes and emotions (Singer & Singer, 1990).

4. A final type of toy or play kit I'd like to emphasize, because of its special role in enhancing narrative and imaginative skills, is the puppet theater. Such playthings were once more widely available to the middle- and upper-class children of European society. A huge collection of these often very artistic and aesthetically impressive children's puppet or marionette theaters is on permanent display in the wonderful Wheelwright Museum of Folk Art in Santa Fe, New Mexico. Perhaps the best-known adults who have mentioned the importance to them of early play with such toys are Goethe, the greatest of German poets and a playwright and theater director; Ibsen, probably the most creative playwright of the nineteenth century; and W. S. Gilbert, the delightful satirist and collaborator with A. S. Sullivan on Britain's finest comic operettas. We cannot expect that all children who are exposed to puppet theaters will move on to such heights of creativity. But we can expect that they will, first of all, enjoy the games for their own sake as they play out various roles and try out different voices and situations. In this way, they can polish their abilities and transform external experience into small-scale, controllable forms, developing their means of storytelling and their narrative thought. Last year, we observed how two of our granddaughters, after listening to an audiotape of *The Phantom of the Opera*, proceeded to my wife's play therapy room and tried to reproduce the opera with their own story variations and music, over and over again, playing

in the puppet theater. Such play can give any ordinary child opportunities to enhance the imagination. The great flexibility in
mental representations of a variety of social scripts and scenarios
can be creative in dozens of later life endeavors. I would propose
that we need more and varied forms of such story-provoking play
kits.

Some concluding remarks

I have ranged widely in this chapter because I believe even cognitive, developmental, and clinical psychologists, not to mention
parents, teachers, and some toy industry executives, do not fully
appreciate the tremendous importance of early imaginative play
as a basis for adaptive thinking processes. Jerome Bruner (1986)
has written wisely and beautifully about what he calls the two
forms of thought, the *paradigmatic* and the *narrative*. The former
represents our ability to think in orderly, logical sequences, the
basis for scientific analysis and communication; the latter represents our ability to mirror events, to form them into stories, and
to create possible worlds for inner play or for practical anticipations of social situations. I propose that the early make-believe of
children is the starting point for the development of narrative
thought. With the proper environment, parental acceptance, play-
fulness, storytelling, and reading, and with the availability of some
kinds of toys, children can sharpen their capacities for narrative
thought. As they do so, they can enjoy childhood more fully and
later, as adults, reap the benefits of a wide-ranging imaginative
capacity.

2

Play, toys, and language

ANTHONY D. PELLEGRINI AND ITHEL JONES

The language that children use when they play with toys is interesting to parents, teachers, and researchers. At one level, each of these groups is interested in the play and language children use with specific toys. For example, parents and teachers may choose specific toys for their children to play with because of the types of play and language that they think the toys will elicit. Specific toys may be purchased because of their potential educational value. Similarly, researchers often examine the effects of specific toys, such as war toys, on children's play (see Sutton-Smith, 1992 and this volume, and Smith et al., 1992 and this volume). These views of the effects of toys generally take the position that the toys themselves elicit the play and language that are observed. In the language of ecological psychologists like Barker and Wright (1955) and Gump (1989), the environment, of which toys are part, "coerces" behaviors from individuals; children, from this perspective, have minimal influence on the environment.

A contrasting view, dating back at least to Kurt Lewin (1954) and more recently to Bronfenbrenner (1979), conceptualizes the environment and toys more specifically in transactional terms. By *transaction* we mean that children and toys influence each other. The ways in which children interact with specific toys vary ac-

The first author was partially supported by a grant from the National Reading Research Center to the University of Georgia.

cording to features of the children themselves, such as temperament, gender, and age, and of the toys themselves; the toys do not elicit the behavior independently of characteristics of the child. Children, as they interact with adults and each other around a specific toy, define the meaning of the toy for that particular situation. The meaning of the toy changes, depending on the value assigned to it by the players. Scarcity/availability of other toys in the environment, and other resources such as available play time, affect the meaning assigned to toys.

In this chapter we first briefly outline two contrasting views of toys as context: toys having unidirectional and transactional effects. Our discussion will be confined to children's play and language with toys in preschool settings because this is the age group and setting with which most of the research on play, language, and toys has been conducted. Second, we discuss the ways in which play and language vary according to the specific types of toys and the social environments in which they are embedded. Lastly, we present exploratory data relating to the forms of language used by children as they try to gain access to and maintain possession of toys that they value or don't value.

Toys as context

Toys can be presented as part of a coercive environment (Gump, 1989) such that the toys, as part of the larger environment, elicit specific behaviors. This unidirectional view of toys – that is, that toys affect children's play – is rooted in an ecological psychology tradition that minimizes the work of individuals in redefining their roles in specific environments. For example, Roger Barker (1968) used an atoms–molecule metaphor to describe the role of individuals in specific contexts: Just as atoms are controlled by molecules, so too are individual participants controlled in specific environments. Applying this metaphor to toys, play, and language, the following scenario can be predicted: Preschool girls playing with

Barbie dolls will use language that is consistent with a Barbie role. For example:

> *Child (C) 1:* "Her hair is beautiful."
> *C2:* "Yeah, but she really should go to get it done again."
> *C1:* "Yeah. She can get her nails done too."
> *C2:* "And maybe a new dress."

The obvious point here is that Barbie dolls should elicit gender-stereotypic play and language.

An alternative view of the environment generally and toys specifically is that players, in their interactions with each other and with toys, often redefine the nature of the toys. We suggest that children's interactions with specific toys, rather than being defined by the physical props themselves, are a result of the ways in which the participants themselves define the toys. That definition varies according to the children's age and the nature of the social group playing with the toys. For example, play with Barbie dolls between a boy and one of the girls from the preceding hypothetical example would probably differ from the preceding scenario between two girls. The boys would probably interact minimally with such a toy. Indeed, they would probably do so only reluctantly; we would not hear much speech from them, and what speech is heard might be oppositional, such as "That's pretty dumb." The girl's play may, correspondingly, be different from her earlier play with another girl. Whereas her play with the other girl may be reciprocal (i.e., alternating relatively equal roles), her play with the boy may be complementary (trying to elicit the boy's play or guiding it).

At a more macro-contextual level, children from various cultural backgrounds will play with Barbie dolls in different ways. For example, some white preschoolers in the southeastern United States are discouraged from engaging in fantasy play about specific fictional characters (Heath, 1983). Similarly, black preschool girls may only reluctantly play with Barbie (McLoyd, 1982). Indeed, daughters of parents who discourage gender-stereotyped behavior would probably play with Barbie differently than daughters of parents advocating more traditional gender roles.

The point here is that the relation between toys and play is not as simple as it may first appear. We believe that the types of play and language children use with certain toys and in certain social groups is related to children's desire to gain and maintain access to those toys. That is, we treat toys as resources that children either value or don't value. When children play with toys of high value, they should be highly motivated to sustain play and, consequently, will utilize varied and often sophisticated linguistic strategies to gain access to toys they value.

Play and language with toys in preschool contexts

Parents and teachers of preschoolers, as well as researchers, have for many years recognized that certain toy/social configurations motivate children to engage in specific activities. Children tend to exhibit high levels of competence when they interact with valued toys and with peers/adults simply because they are motivated to participate (Pellegrini & Perlmutter, 1989). If sustained play requires sophisticated language, children will be motivated to use it as a way to maintain play. Thus, it is not accidental that researchers asking children to complete a research task often ask the children to "play a game" with them. Vygotsky (1967) must certainly have recognized this phenomenon when he suggested that during fantasy play children often exhibit a higher level of competence than they do in nonplay.

The language of play

The language that children use to initiate and sustain fantasy play, that is, the language used to serve an imaginative function, is characterized by specific linguistic features (Halliday, 1969–70). These features, in turn, are considered important to children's

Table 2.1. *Halliday's functions of language*

Function	Definition	Example
Instrumental	Satisfy one's needs	I want that.
Regulatory	Control others	Get that.
Interactional	Define/consolidate	Let's be friends.
Personal	Express feelings	I like her.
Heuristic	Explore the world	Why's that so?
Imaginative	Create make-believe	I'll be Daddy.
Representational	Convey information	It's black.

subsequent communicative competence in a variety of school and community settings (Hymes, 1971). By *communicative competence* we mean that children have a varied linguistic repertoire and are capable of using appropriate forms in different speech events. For example, a mark of communicative competence is that a child's directions to his or her home for a person not familiar with the area should be marked by additive conjunctions (such as *and*) and linguistically defined pronouns and demonstratives; directions to peers familiar with the area may be more reliant on shared knowledge (e.g., "It's next to the pie shop") than on verbal encoding of meaning (e.g., "The third house of the south side of Morton Road"). Indeed, fantasy play is a particularly good venue for allowing children to learn a varied repertoire of linguistic strategies (Halliday, 1969–70; Pellegrini, 1983). In fantasy, children take on a variety of roles, some of which they cannot take on in real life; thus, fantasy affords an opportunity to learn and practice a variety of ways in which to use language.

An interesting model for categorizing the ways in which children use language to serve a variety of functions has been developed by Halliday (1969–70). Halliday's seven functions of language, with corresponding examples, are displayed in Table 2.1. Children's facility with these different functions is an indicator of their ability to use language to serve a variety of purposes and, consequently, a good measure of communicative competence. Children capable of using more functions should be considered more communicatively competent than those capable of using fewer functions. Correspondingly, the ability to embed more than one function in single utterances results in advanced syntax.

Another important feature of the language children use during social fantasy play is its decontextualized nature. By *decontextualized* we mean the language that conveys meaning, primarily through lexical and syntactic means; reliance on contextual cues and shared information to convey meaning is minimized. For example, decontextualized language involves using language to define a play theme or to redefine a toy. This language variant, or *register,* is characterized by linguistically defined pronouns, elaborated nominal groups (e.g., adjectives used to elaborate nouns), and use of various conjunctions (e.g., *if, then, but, and, then*) for organization.

Contextualized language is the opposite: linguistically undefined pronouns and little if any nominal elaboration and conjunction use. Although meaning can be conveyed successfully through either form, the latter relies on context, such as pointing, and/or shared knowledge.

The distinction between contextualized and decontextualized language is particularly important in schooling. Opportunities to use language to redefine play props and toys enable children to develop the ability to have one representational medium, language, represent something else. This representational competence is obviously important in school-based literacy learning. In schools children are expected to use decontextualized forms of language in their oral lesson recitations, as well as in comprehending and producing decontextualized texts in reading and writing lessons (e.g., Cook-Gumperz, 1977). In both reading and writing, children must learn that words, like fantasy play transformations, are meaningful representations of something else.

The final aspect of fantasy play language to be considered is the language children use as they attempt to gain access to and maintain possession of certain toys and play themes. This form of language, because it often involves disputes and persuasions, shares features with the language of conflict. The work of Catherine

Garvey (1991; in press) is particularly relevant, as she has carefully described the forms of language that children use as they negotiate conflicts and disagreements in the course of fantasy play. Conflicts, "broken" play episodes, and subsequent renegotiation, clarification, and compromise are frequent occurrences in fantasy play (Garvey, 1987; Pellegrini, 1982; Sachs, Goldman & Chailé, 1984; Wolf & Grollman, 1982).

Conflicts can arise for a number of reasons. First, they may occur because of the ambiguity inherent in fantasy (i.e., real objects and people typically have different meanings in fantasy) or because a player wants to change the course of the fantasy episode. Conflicts may also arise because of access to toys and/or enactment of a preferred play theme. Whatever the cause, conflicts are typically resolved by children because they enjoy the playful interaction and want it to continue. In short, the ambiguous characteristics inherent in social fantasy and its motivating power enable children to pose and resolve conflicts with peers. The talk that is used by children in conflicts surrounding social pretense, according to Garvey (1987), is characterized by maintenance of the fantasy orientation and proposals of alternative themes and rules. Conflictual interaction outside of the fantasy frame is also characterized by rules and conventions, but these are based in the real world, not in a fantasy theme. Indeed, if we treat access to toys and preferred play themes as a subset of more general resources to be acquired, we see that children use similar strategies; for example, they can use force, deception, and reason to gain access (Charlesworth, 1988). Use of such conflict resolution strategies, in turn, is important in children's development to the extent that they are reliable indicators of social cognitive status (e.g., Pellegrini & Perlmutter, 1988).

Social fantasy may afford an important venue through which children learn to reflect on socially shared meaning and the ways meaning can change as they interact with others. Conflicts inherent in social fantasy, along with other self-reflective processes, such as the realization that the physical appearance of an object and its social meaning can differ, are probably important components in children's ability to understand the ways in which different people view the same event (Harris, 1990).

Play and language with toys in preschool classrooms

A fair amount of research has been conducted on the forms of play and language children use while interacting with various props and toys in their preschool classrooms. In this section we discuss some of our work in this area.

Toys' effects

This research, for the most part, found that children's play and language tend to follow the themes suggested by the toys or props themselves (e.g., Quiltich & Risley, 1973). This was especially true of functionally explicit or realistic toys having a clear function, such as a doctor's kit or a truck. Not surprisingly, when children choose to play with functionally explicit toys, their play and language follow the themes suggested by the toys. When they choose to play with toys offering a fantastic theme, such as dolls or dinosaurs, their play is fantastic and their language is decontextualized rather than contextualized. When they play with props suggesting a more realistic play mode, such as constructive toys, play is less imaginative and more constructive, and their language tends to be more contextualized than decontextualized (Pellegrini, 1982, 1983). The position stated in these chapters is that in order to initiate and maintain fantasy play, children must use decontextualized language to the extent that their play is fantastic. Fantasy, because of the lack of correspondence between reality and the theme being enacted (e.g., a child could be a doctor or a villain in play), requires explicit language in order for players to understand the play theme.

The ambiguity that typically accompanies such play has two possible consequences. The play episode may end immediately because the ambiguity is such that players cannot reach mutual understanding. Although some fantasy episodes do end this way, there is often an intermediate phase wherein children try to clarify the ambiguity by asking directly (e.g., "What's that mean?") or indirectly for explication (such as by repeating the ambiguous theme with a questioning intonation: "A car?"). The result of such clarification sequences, even when the play ends rather quickly, is that children attempt to explicate, with decontextualized language, the meaning of their play statements. Children seem to be motivated to explicate their themes because they enjoy the fantasy that will ensue.

An example will illustrate the process: Two preschool girls were playing with water, jars, and cooking utensils in their school when one, Chloe, took a plastic jar, dipped it in the sink filled with soapy water, shook the filled jar until suds came flowing, handed it to Lila, and asked: "Chocolate or vanilla?" Lila, looking puzzled, repeated Chloe's utterance, but with a questioning intonation: "Chocolate or vanilla?" Lila seemingly wanted the play to continue because she responded to Chloe's utterance, but she did not know the meaning of the utterance because of the sudsy mess she was being given. Chloe, being communicatively competent, clarified the ambiguity: "Chocolate or vanilla ice cream. Do you want some?" Chloe explicated the meaning of her ambiguous ellipsis, and the play continued.

Children's use of different functions of language also varies according to the toys they choose to play with. In one classroom observational study, 2-, 3-, and 4-year-olds use of different functions of language was compared in play centers containing realistic housekeeping toys, such as toy pots, pans, stoves, and refrigerators, and art materials, such as paper, pens/pencils/crayons, scissors, glue, and water/sand tables (Pellegrini, 1983). Children used more varied functions of language in the housekeeping centers than in the others; correspondingly, their individual utterances in reference to these fantasy props served more varied functions. Children playing with blocks used more imaginative language and multifunctional utterances than when playing with art materials. When children played with art materials they generally did so in a solitary, not a social, manner; consequently, they did not use much language with such materials.

The explanation for these results seems rather simple. The ambiguity inherent in fantasy elicits decontextualized language. Children engage in the rather strenuous cognitive work of verbal explication because fantasy is something they enjoy. These results support the idea that children who choose to play with fantastic toys use imaginative and varied language.

Children sometimes do this with constructive toys such as blocks. When children play with functionally ambiguous toys like blocks, they construct their own fantasy themes. This process is unlike the reliance on the play themes suggested in the functionally explicit props. It is not surprising that preschool children engage in fantasy with ambiguous props because, by 4 years of age, children are capable of symbolic transformations independent of prop structure (Fein, 1981; McLoyd, 1982; Pellegrini, 1987).

It has been suggested that the social context of playing with blocks is important in influencing the form of play that children exhibit; when children play with blocks alone their play has been characterized as constructive, but when they play with a peer it has been characterized as fantastic (Rubin, Fein & Vandenberg, 1983). Although social context is clearly important, it also may be the case that researchers code play as fantastic when it is social because children playing in groups are more likely to use language, compared to when they play alone, thus making the fantasy more obvious (Vygotsky, 1962). Children's solitary play with blocks may be fantastic, but if they do not talk about it, observers have difficulty knowing that, so they code it as constructive rather than fantastic.

Naturalistic studies of fantasy and language with toys in classroom settings, such as those previously described, are important not only because they describe what children do in their everyday world but also because they inform us about the value children place on different toys; toys played with more frequently by a variety of children are obviously more valuable to them than toys played with less frequently.

Considering the effects of dramatic play props (e.g., doctors' kits) and constructive props (e.g., wooden and plastic blocks) on children's uses of language, we find, not surprisingly, that more imaginative language is observed in reference to doctors' kits (Pellegrini, 1983). This is especially the case for older (5-year-old) children compared to younger (4-year-old) children (Pellegrini, 1986). It is probable that linguistic maturity is required to interact fully in a social context around toys requiring fantasy. This seems to be the case even when the toys are relatively realistic doctors' kits.

When children play with realistic toys, they use the same forms of decontextualized language that characterize their play in naturalistic settings. That is, play with functionally explicit toys, compared to play with functionally ambiguous toys, was characterized by children verbally encoding meaning (Pellegrini, 1986) and by their weaving longer narrative play themes (Pellegrini, 1987a). Realistic toys help to "scaffold" older children's use of decontextualized language. They may use realistic toys as a basis from which to engage in fantasy themes related to but not dependent on the toys themselves. Play with doctors' kits entailed not only talking about the dolls and the doctors' instruments that were present but also talking about related, though physically absent, phenomena. For example, two girls talked about feeding a doll using imaginary food, plates, and utensils; bathing it in an imaginary tub with imaginary soap and sponge; and then taking it to the doctor, where their talk centered on the props. By way of evidence for these claims regarding realistic toys compared to less structured toys, children used classes of words that represent physically absent phenomena (e.g., third-person pronouns, past and future tense verbs) (Pellegrini, 1986), and their play themes were longer and more integrated (Pellegrini, 1985).

The realistic props compared to the ambiguous props may lessen information processing demands, so that children can go beyond the physically present props. Play centered on the ambiguous props was "fractured," characterized by short, disrupted play themes. This suggests that children may have difficulty defining a play theme jointly and sustaining it. Thus, children of different ages play with realistic and ambiguous toys in different ways. When they play with realistic toys, their play relates to the theme of the toys and is more context bound. Play episodes with these toys, however, are long and involved. In contrast, play with less realistic props tends to be more varied, and the language surrounding this play is more decontextualized; in addition, the individual play episodes with ambiguous toys tend to be shorter.

Social mediators of toys

As we noted earlier, toys are only one dimension of context; when different participants play with toys, children probably redefine the ways in which the toys can be used. At a general level, this is illustrated when we examine the different roles served by peers and adults in mediating children's play and language; the role of participants, in turn, should vary according to age. The different roles of adults and peers in the play of young children form an important development issue. For instance, both Piaget (1983) and Vygotsky (1978) addressed these different roles in their theories of development.

Piaget's theory, especially regarding children's moral development (1965), suggests that children's interaction with peers is reciprocal and that their interaction with adults is complementary. In some areas, like moral development, the former relationship is more likely to spur development. According to this position, adult–child relationships inhibit development because of their unilateral nature: Adults generally tell children what to do, and children generally comply. Peer interaction, on the other hand, is characterized by more reciprocal and negotiated roles; consequently, children take more varied roles and use more varied language. Vygotsky (1978), on the other hand, stressed the role of the adult in promoting children's development. The language strategies that adults and children negotiate in the course of development are appropriated by children to guide their future behavior.

These conceptualizations are obviously oversimplifications. Not all adult–child relationships are complementary, and not all peer relationships are reciprocal. When one child teaches another how to play a game, the relationship is complementary. When fathers and sons engage in rough-and-tumble play, the roles are reciprocal. Other relevant factors in the social context include individual differences and prior interactional history (Hinde, 1976). The ways in which people interact with each other are, in turn, affected by the materials, such as toys, they interact around. As such, the roles of adults and peers in regard to children's cognition, language, and play are not simple. Peers and adults differentially affect children's development, depending on the age of the children and the specific situation in which they are observed. In convergent tasks, like route planning, adults are more effective than children in facilitating preschoolers' effective strategies (Tudge & Rogoff, 1989).

In more divergent situations, like fantasy play, the complementary interactions that typify most teacher–student relationships often inhibit sophisticated fantasy. The reciprocal style characteristic of many peer relationships facilitates social fantasy. These interaction styles, however, vary with the age of the children. With very young children, adults provide the support necessary for them to take a role in play episodes. Specifically, we find in naturalistic observations in preschool classrooms that with 2-year-olds, the number of teachers present is positively and significantly correlated with children's linguistic facility, that is, their use of numerous functions of language (Pellegrini, 1983). The infant or toddler, in short, is dependent on a caregiver for a number of social and material services; this is a characteristic of the period of prolonged childhood typifying our species.

With older children (from about 3½ years of age on), however, teachers' presence seems to inhibit fantasy play (Pellegrini, 1984) and corresponding imaginative and multifunctional language (Pellegrini, 1983). For these older children, on the other hand, most sophisticated forms of play and uses of language occur in the presence of peers, not adults (Pellegrini, 1983). It may be that adults help very young children to engage in social play by teaching them the strategies necessary to engage in social fantasy, such as turn taking and verbal encoding of ambiguous aspects of play that must be clarified if play is to continue. These results suggest that by the time children are 3 years of age, however, adults inhibit social fantasy and corresponding forms of language, whereas peers facilitate them (Pellegrini & Perlmutter, 1989).

The experimental literature is consistent with these naturalistic findings. Specifically, parents facilitate younger children's fantasy, whereas peers facilitate the verbal fantasy of older children (5½ years of age) (Perlmutter & Pellegrini, 1987). Interestingly, Perlmutter and Pellegrini found that the verbal fantasy generated in the peer context related to children's social perspective taking, whereas the fantasy with parents generally, did not. It may be the case, following Piaget (1965), that fantasy with peers, compared to that with adults, is typified by conceptual conflict and accommodation to differing points of view. On the other hand, it may be the case that repeated social fantasy typified by reciprocal interaction with a familiar playmate, like a sibling or an adult, facilitates social cognition. The self-reflection characteristic of such interactions may be responsible for sensitivity to different social perspectives (Dunn, 1988; Harris, 1990).

In our group of middle-class parents, there were no gender differences in the ways in which parents played with their children. This is interesting in light of Block's suggestion that fathers are more demanding than mothers. Perhaps gender difference is "channelized" by exposure to specific props (Eisenberg, Wolchik, Hernandez & Pasternack, 1985). Also, middle-class parents may recognize the demand characteristics of experimental play situations and minimize gender differences that might ordinarily occur in the home. Only research using longer and more frequent observation, with controlled toys presented in the home, can answer this question.

Toys as resources

The forms of play and language that children exhibit with various toys are influenced by both social and material factors. As noted earlier, peers and adults, with their reciprocal and complementary interaction styles, interact with different toys in different ways.

It may be useful to consider the value of toys along a continuum from highly valued to not valued. One way of determining the extent to which a specific toy is valued is by observing how frequently it is played with. If two children assign high value to the toys that they are interacting with, they will probably enjoy playing with each other and, consequently, be motivated to interact around the toys.

Children play longer and in more complex ways when they interact in same-gender groups and with gender-preferred toys (see Huston, 1983, and Rubin et al., 1983, for reviews). It is probably the case that valued toys and social groups elicit complex play and language because children are motivated to interact with peers around preferred toys. That children are motivated to participate in these settings is, in turn, responsible for their using the language forms necessary to introduce and maintain fantasy play. Thus, children seem to value fantasy play with same-gender playmates and expend considerable cognitive and linguistic resources, for example, to negotiate the conflicts inherent in these episodes.

In the remainder of this chapter, we discuss the specific forms of language that children use as they interact with toys of varying value. We present a typology of the forms of language that boys and girls in same-sex pairs exhibit while playing with two sets of toys provided for them. Children still had to engage their peers with these toys. We regard the social fantasy thus created between peers as a resource. The strategies available to children to secure resources include threats and aggression, deception, manipulation, and cooperation (Charlesworth, 1988). Following reciprocal altruism theory (Trivers, 1971), we assume that cooperation will be a dominant strategy because these children were in the same classroom and would continue to interact. In cases where participants repeatedly interact with each other, cooperation, rather than cheating or aggression, is typically a more effective strategy to acquire resources (Axelrod & Hamilton, 1981; Trivers, 1971).

The children in this study were part of an ongoing research project whose aim was to explicate context–play relations. Although specific details are available elsewhere (Pellegrini & Perlmutter, 1989), some general information is necessary here. The 4- and 5-year-old children all attended the laboratory preschool at the University of Georgia and were primarily from highly educated families. The data from five female and four male pairs were included for analysis here. These children were observed playing in a laboratory playroom in their preschool in same-age and same-gender dyads across four separate 15-min periods: twice with male-preferred blocks and twice with gender-neutral doctors' kits.

Children's play was videotaped through a one-way mirror; their language and corresponding nonverbal behaviors were transcribed verbatim. These utterances were first classified as either fantastic or realistic. Next, all utterances were classified according to the way in which they were used to introduce, maintain, or change play themes. A total of 47 separate codes accounted for all utterances. These codes were then collapsed into the six categories in Table 2.2.

Rather than treating individual children within each pair as the unit of analysis, the dyad itself was considered the unit of analysis. The reasoning is straightforward: Individual children's play and language within a dyad are interdependent, and to consider them as independent makes little sense.

Using language to introduce and maintain play with gender-typed toys

Not surprisingly, girls were significantly more likely than boys to engage in fantasy and use fantasy-oriented language. Actually, girls also engaged in fantasy more frequently than boys with both the

Table 2.2. *Instrumental fantasy language*

Category	Definition	Example
1. Aggression	Tries to hurt other	You jerk!
2. Verbal dominance	Takes charge	I'll be the doctor.
3. Deception	Misleads other	That's mine.
4. Rough play	Weapon play/play fight	I'll shoot you.
5. Negotiates	Compromises	Can I have it now?
6. Rules	Normative behavior	First you, then me.

Note: 1. Aggression, physical dominance: composed of grabs/takes, kicks/hits/pushes, calls names. 2. Verbal dominance: takes preferred role, establishes goal, proposes alternative, directs attention. 3. Deception/guilt: explicitly excludes other, guilt/blame. 4. Rough play: vigorous play, weapon play. 5. Negotiates: asks for toy, offers other toy, assigns or offers preferred role, asks for consent, asks other for definition. 6. Rules: gives rationale, promises, normative comparisons, truth value.

male-preferred and neutral toys. This finding is consistent with much previous research suggesting such gender differences. It may be the case, however, that girls continue to exhibit high levels of fantasy, even with male-preferred toys, only when they play with other girls, not with boys. Cross-gender play actually inhibits girls' exhibition of competence with both neutral and male-preferred toys (Pellegrini & Perlmutter, 1989). Thus, it is important to consider toys and social participants jointly.

Next, we looked at *aggression* and found, like others, that children exhibited very low levels of aggression and that these rates did not vary by gender or toy context. Although there were some instances of children transforming the props into various make-believe weapons, such as swords, guns, and rockets, these incidents did not result in subsequent aggression. It may be that children treat play with toy guns and such as play, not as aggression (Sutton-Smith, 1992). Other factors, such as parental use of corporal punishment, may be better predictors of aggression than play with toy guns (Watson & Peng, 1992). Of course, the present research venue, a laboratory playroom in a preschool, probably suppressed children's exhibition of aggression to the extent that they knew they were being closely observed. This interpretation is supported by the related finding that both boys and girls in both contexts exhibited low levels of verbal dominance utterances. The low levels of aggression and verbal dominance are also consistent with the theory of reciprocal altruism, in which cooperation, not aggression, would be a preferred strategy among children who meet repeatedly. The subsequent results support this logic.

Verbal negotiations were used 179 times where *verbal dominance* and *aggression* were exhibited 111 and 9 times, respectively. Further, girls exhibited more verbal negotiations than boys, despite the toys, whereas boys seemed to negotiate more while playing with the male-preferred toys. It is probably the case that having children play with toys that are preferred or neutral facilitates their willingness to compromise and negotiate with other children. It may be that sharing is facilitated when playing with preferred toys because children know they will be encountering the same children repeatedly. That is not to say that children may not argue or fight over access to toys, especially if there is a limited number of toys. They probably do this less often, however, with children, like friends, with whom they interact repeatedly.

In short, children seem to use very different forms of fantasy language when they play with different toys. When the toys are preferred, children exhibit sophisticated verbal interaction strategies to introduce and maintain play. The extent to which a toy is gender-stereotyped appears to be a reasonably good guide to children's preference for that toy.

Conclusion

The ways in which children play with specific toys is not a simple matter. The forms of play that children exhibit varies according to the types of toys and playmates. Children seem to exhibit most sophisticated forms of play when they interact with toys they value and with children and adults they will encounter repeatedly.

We also suggest that researchers consider toys and the social environment as part of a contextual matrix influencing children's behavior, development, and learning. Hinde's (1976) notion of relationships is particularly useful. Briefly, contexts are organized such that individual differences influence interaction, which, in turn, influences long-term relationships. These interaction patterns vary according to the age of the child and the environment of which he or she is a part. The play that children and adults exhibit with specific toys should be relevant to those individuals in their specific niches. Children's choice of specific toys and the ways in which they play with those toys will vary with local conditions.

3
Educational toys, creative toys

BIRGITTA ALMQVIST

The terms *educational toys* and *creative toys* are related in the sense that they both attribute human qualities to inanimate objects. Although no one with common sense believes that an object, by itself, can teach or that other inanimate objects can be creative all by themselves, the classification has caused much misunderstanding, not least because it suggests a polarization; the opposite of an educational toy would be a noneducational toy, which would inhibit learning, and the opposite of a creative toy would be a noncreative toy, which would suppress creativity. In fact, this interpretation is often used, particularly by teachers and parents. This chapter examines the background as well as the consequences of the labels *educational toys* and *creative toys* and discusses, on the basis of international research on children and toys, various aspects of the function of toys in children's learning and fantasy play.

The rebirth of the educational toy

It is important to note that the label *educational toy* is by no means a new invention. The purpose of toys has practically always been educational. The bows and arrows that little boys in ancient Rome were given to play with were undoubtedly regarded as vehicles for training future warrior mastery. And when the children of a peasant culture played family – the boys with farming tools and hunting

weapons and the girls with wooden log dolls and miniature cooking utensils – they were supposed to practice their future adult
roles in the society. Although dolls are still regarded as appropriate
for girls, today such boys' toys as bows and arrows and the like
are called *war toys* or *toys conducive to violence.*

To practice future adult roles by imitating them in play was
regarded as an exclusive pastime in the old days. Practice came
naturally for the boy when he worked side by side with his father
hunting and farming and for the girl when she helped her mother
in the kitchen or looked after younger sisters and brothers, which
today is still the case in certain cultures.

In *Toys as Culture*, Brian Sutton-Smith (1986) gives a historical
account of the attitudes toward play and toys over the centuries,
and it is from that account I have chosen the following items to
illustrate what I call the *educational toy tradition.*

It is interesting to note that up to the seventeenth century the
word toy was synonymous with "any petty commodity, a thing
of no great value," reflecting the attitudes toward toys. One who
may be given credit for a changed attitude toward toys at that
time was the English philosopher John Locke, who claimed that
toys and play could be used in the education of young children.
Locke even produced a toy, a set of letter blocks that was meant
not only to teach children the alphabet. As Locke wished to please
an emerging middle class, the main purpose of his letter blocks
was to make middle-class sons and daughters stay indoors and
play instead of running about in the streets. My guess is that
Locke's blocks were intended principally for boys, as the very idea
that middle-class girls would be running about in the streets must
have seemed absurd. The middle-class girl, whose future it was to
be a faithful housewife, was probably expected to stay in her room
and play with her Nüremberg cabinet house, a doll's house with
which young ladies could learn how to run a household (King,
1978). Rather than teaching children specific skills, however, these
educational devices became "an incentive to keep children indoors,
where they could be governed by tutors rather than by their rough
brethren on the streets" (Sutton-Smith, 1986, p. 119).

The first triumphal march of the educational toy took place in the late 1700s. The market offered a "virtual array of educational toys and games that used packs of cards to teach geography, history, spelling and astronomy." To make learning more enticing, the manufacturers advertised their educational devices as "improving toys," but in the pleasurable combination of "entertainment, amusement and instruction."

Besides educational card games there were educational jigsaw puzzles, invented by John Spilsbury in a print shop off Drury Lane in London in the early 1760s (Vandivert & Vandivert, 1974). The Spilsbury invention, the *dissected maps,* as he called them, were meant to teach children geography and became a success from the start. They were quickly copied by others, and a couple of decades later a variety of educational jigsaws, designed to teach children geography, history, and "high morals," appeared. One such jigsaw was described as "Suitable for the Instruction of Youth of all Ages, Designed to impress upon their minds a love to Virtue and a hatred to Vice," and another was "A map of the Various Paths of Life." Probably the intention of the latter was to make children see the bliss of wandering on "the narrow path."

It was not until the nineteenth century that the educational emphasis of toys began to recede. Whether it was due to the opening of an international toy market is difficult to say, but the English and German manufacturers who opened the doors to a more joyful toy market were met by enthusiasm. Now was the era when children – at least those from the middle and upper classes – were given toys to keep as their personal belongings.

> Educational toys were to be the toys of solitariness, a marked shift from all prior usages of miniature objects in magic and in festivals throughout history as well as from all prior forms of play, which had been typically communal in character. Children were coming to be recognized as individuals. (Sutton-Smith, 1986, p. 120)

At the beginning of the nineteenth century, Friedrich Froebel, a German educator, stated that there was a connection between the toy and the child's soul, and that personal development could come about only by expression through appropriate external objects and forms. In this spirit he designed his gifts, which were said to be "gifts from Gods," and which were used in the "divine occupation" of play. Froebel also set up the first kindergarten (in Blankenberg, Thüringen, Germany) and has since had an immense influence on preschool education throughout the world.

With the exception of a few periods (e.g., the Montessori wave in the 1920s), psychologists and educators of our own century have put more emphasis on the personality of the child than on toys. The modal philosophy today is that children should be allowed to develop without straitjackets, and that their needs and abilities should be treated with respect and understanding. Children should be encouraged to play, and they should have access to a variety of toys.

In the late 1960s, however, something occurred that changed the attitudes toward toys and resulted in a continuous conflict between what can be called disparate "toy interest groups." Toys should be educational to stimulate and improve children's intellectual development, and they should be ambiguous and without a fixed purpose, or else children's fantasy will be too directed. As farfetched as it may sound, that the term *educational toys* was met with so much enthusiasm in the 1960s may, in fact, have resulted from the space race between the United States and the Soviet Union some 10 years earlier. The history of the role of play in the school curriculum indicates that the Soviet success with Sputnik was interpreted by the U.S. government as a failure of the schools to teach mathematics and science properly and further indicates that a playless curriculum was required to establish faster-paced learning in the schools (Glickman, 1981). Probably this American school emphasis was one reason for the intensified interest in early childhood education that soon spread to other industrial countries. In Sweden, for example, the most comprehensive preschool reform in the country's history took place in 1968 when it was decided to consolidate all forms of child care for children under school age under the same roof, *förskolan* (a direct translation of the word *preschool*), in which everything was to have an educational purpose, play and toys included.

But the children did not ask primarily for education, at least not in the adult sense of the word. Children of the 1960s and 1970s wanted to play, just like the children before and after them. Either playing is allowed or not, which can be exemplified by the reactions of a group of 5-year-olds whom I asked: "What would you say if someone told you that from now on play is forbidden?" The children first stared at me as if they didn't understand the question, but after a while one little girl spoke up, or rather stammered: "Then I would...like to...," but then changed her tone and resolutely declared: "I wouldn't care, I'd just go on playing."

No doubt children prefer playing over education, which the authors of the Swedish program for preschool education probably were aware of, inasmuch as the program declares that "play is of crucial importance to children in the preschool ages" and therefore should be the predominant educational method. As an educational method, play is supposed to be well structured to contribute to learning. But children do not like it when their play is fenced in all the time. This is wise of them because when play is no longer free and spontaneous, it has lost its playful character. This problem, however, was elegantly solved by inserting daily free-play periods into the preschool program.

As play was to be educational, the toys also had to be educational – except perhaps in the free-play periods. However, not all toys were considered educational, and it became necessary to separate the mere trifles from the educational toys and label them accordingly. The label *educational toy* was reserved for toys that were plain in structure, texture, form, and color and gender-neutral to suit girls as well as boys. Therefore, I would argue that the late 1960s was the time for the rebirth of the educational toy, an exquisite "baby" that was welcomed and cherished by parents as well as preschool teachers (and toy manufacturers, for that matter) throughout the 1970s and well into the 1980s. Later I will argue that, although the aura has somewhat faded, it is still fully visible.

As I noted earlier, the toy manufacturers of the twentieth century did not oppose the rebirth of the educational toy. Rather, they were as ardent as were their forerunners 200 years earlier. Enthusiastically, and possibly in good faith, they announced that educational toys would not only improve children's learning (or often specific skills) but also increase their intelligence. No wonder these promising devices were met with open arms, both by preschool teachers with the ambition to use toys as teaching tools in the children's play and by parents with the ambition to give their offspring the best possible start in school. The success gave way to a flow of educational toys on the market, and from 1965 on, the sale of so-called educational toys increased from about 4% to about 15% over less than 10 years (Quilitch, 1974).

However, by attaching the label *educational toys* to a specific segment of its production, the toy industry created a dilemma for itself, because if the other toys produced were not educational, what were they? Noneducational? Mere trifles for joy? The latter kind of toy was often regarded with dismay by teachers and – in their wake – parents of young children. Toys that were not labeled educational were vain mayflies, "trendies" that symbolized shallowness and therefore were assumed to have a bad influence on children.

Educational toys were given much higher status than other toys. Educational toys should have certain qualities to teach children certain skills (in line with what is anticipated by the school curriculum, only not quite as elaborate) and should therefore be "serious" and plain so that they do not lure children to play with them just for the fun of it. Play was not only to be taken seriously, it was to be serious. The exception was during periods of free play, typically interpreted as "free from teacher involvement," when the children usually were (and still are) left alone.

That the romanticism of the educational toy faded was due to the children's own reactions toward it. As children found the educational toys dull, they just stepped over them and went searching for more joyful playthings. And a toy that no child wants to play with is not much use, however educational it is supposed to be. Manufacturers of today seem to have realized that labeling toys as educational is rather pointless and have instead begun to advertise them as toys that can inspire the child to learning something and to strengthen the child's self-esteem. The Swedish company BRIO, in one advertisement, makes a joke of the attitudes of the educational toy generation as opposed to those of an older generation that bothered very little about the educational value of toys: Grandmother has bought little Niklas a toy. Her son, Niklas's daddy, exclaims: "Fine! With this toy, Niklas can improve his logical thinking and develop his organizing skill." To which Grandmother replies: "Fancy that! And I bought it just because it seemed amusing."

Earlier, I claimed that the educational toy is still fully visible. The basis of my statement is an investigation of toys and play materials to which children have access in Swedish child-care institutions. The main finding was that the dominant types of playthings in the institutions (the records indicated a striking homogeneity throughout the country) were educational – art materials such as paper and pencils, clay, crayons, and so on. In addition, toys for playing traffic, farming, shop, and hospital were quite numerous, whereas equipment for playing police, detective, and space men was practically nonexistent. Furthermore, the results are similar to those of a French study (Brougère, 1985) in regard to both homogeneity and types of play materials. It is reasonable to believe that the selection of toys and play materials in a preschool institution not only reflects the teachers' toy preferences but also indicates their play preferences. If so, the toys found in the Swedish and French preschools support the assumption that teachers may in fact prefer "a quiet classroom with concentration on particular activities. Noisy games of space monsters can disrupt this" (Smith, 1983). I don't know about the gender division of preschool teachers in other countries, but in Sweden 96% of them are women. Some of them have told me that they find the boys' rough-and-tumble play most disturbing.

The finding that educational art objects overshadowed all other play materials found in the preschools is not surprising. Toys in an educational context, it is proposed, connote learning, cognition, stimulation, exploration, mastery, performance, and achievement. In a family context, toys mean gifts, exchanges, festivals, bonding, obligation, and "solitarization." It would therefore be assumed that the toys children play with at home are different from those they play with in the preschool.

Apparently, however, it seems that parents, like teachers, place major emphasis on toys as educational. Research data indicate that young children spend at least half of their playing time daily with educational art objects (Giddings & Halverson, 1981; Sutton-Smith, 1986).

What do educational toys have that others don't have?

The educational toy era of the 1970s is somewhat reflected in the literature; nearly half of the more than 300 research reports on children and toys published between 1970 and 1979 concern educational toys, or toys as teaching devices in the education of children (Almqvist, 1989b). None of these reports, however, supports the assumption that so-called educational toys are more educational than others; instead, in virtually all cases, the learning effects have been due to factors other than the toys themselves. In some cases, the adults' engagement in and guiding of the children's toy play have been the crucial factors (Vagt & Müller, 1976). In other cases, the learning improvements have been more strongly related to the children's level of intellectual capacity than to the toys. A study that exemplifies the latter situation (Roeder & Masendorf, 1979) is one in which children with more or less severe learning problems were trained with play materials classified as being either playlike or exerciselike. What is interesting is that, though no overall learning effects were obtained from either type of toy, the results indicated that children with mild learning problems were more stimulated by exerciselike materials and that children with severe learning problems were more stimulated by playlike materials.

One goal of schooling today undoubtedly is to prepare children for a future in a more and more technologically advanced society. Once again, the contemporary society is reflected in the research literature. Most research carried out in the 1980s concerning the use of toys in education focused on teaching natural science, mathematics, and spatial concepts. But this time, findings indicate that some toys more than others can stimulate children's understanding of scientific, mathematical, and spatial concepts, namely, construction toys. It is, however, well documented that children's toy preferences are sex-typed throughout childhood. Girls typically prefer dolls and household items, whereas boys generally prefer action toys. These differences in toy preferences are in line with the socialization of children. Boys are socialized to an outer sphere characterized, for example, by career anticipation, political interests, and cross-cutting associational ties, whereas the socialization of girls goes to an inner sphere where family and domestic matters and child care are the most important issues of life (Richardson & Simpson, 1982). In addition, it is well known that boys often pretend that they are involved in exciting adventures, whereas girls' play takes place on the home ground, so to speak, and their play can be described as "peaceful and domestic." Since such different play scenes obviously demand different verbal skills, the best are taken by the boys. Girls either play mother-and-child or pretend to be princesses or film stars; they simply repeat what they have heard adult females say, which is a reproducing process leading to nothing but verbal fluency. For boys' adventure play on "alien grounds" it is not quite so easy; they may darken their voices to try to sound like Daddy (who represents adult males in general), but Daddy's conversation is far too prosaic for a strange adventure, so the boys have to invent "new lines": What do astronauts talk about up there on the moon? What does a police officer say when confronted with a thief, and what does the scoundrel say in turn?

My proposal that the differences in boys' and girls' play lead to differences in creative language is supported by a study of children's novel responses to toys; as the boys were less stereotyped in their responses than the girls were, it may in fact be that play is more likely to have this utility for boys than for girls (Sutton-Smith, 1968).

It has also been suggested that children who play with boys' toys are given a better opportunity than children who play with girls' toys to develop scientific understanding, mathematical concepts, and spatial skills (Tracy, 1987). But in addition, little girls are not supposed to learn science. The Swedish educational preschool program declares that, because children today are surrounded by technical devices, older children (5- to 6-year-olds) should be given the opportunity to experiment with concrete experiences to gain their first knowledge of the simple techniques they encounter in their everyday lives.

However, there are other things in life worth learning besides science, and any toy can be used by the child as a learning device as long as it facilitates what the child wants to learn. I suggest a classic, like a teddy bear, or trendy toys like a space robot, a Barbie doll, or a Mutant Ninja Turtle, in spite of the fact that none of them would fit into the category of educational toys. But then, whether something is a toy or an instructional object is a decision that rests with the child (Vandenberg, 1987).

Primary-grade children who were participating in a reading project were asked to bring their own teddy bears to school in order to "teach Teddy to read" (Orr, 1976). Although it is doubtful whether teddy actually learned to read, his owners certainly improved their own reading. The reason for the successful outcome seems to be that the children were simultaneously both teachers and learners, which made it easier for them to verbalize reading problems from both points of view.

Teddy turns up in another school program, a creative language arts program in which a teddy bears' "picnic" was arranged to improve first-grade children's verbal skills. Although the teddy bears apparently inspired their owners to tell stories, and to learn "bear songs" and "bear poetry," the following conclusion indicates that perhaps the teacher got the best of it: "As the stories unfolded, I learned much about the boys and girls in my class, as bears had a way of assuming their owners personalities" (Wilczak, 1976).

Ten-year-old Arthur spent all his pocket money on space robot models. As soon as he completed one, he returned to the store to buy another. On being asked what he did when he was not busy building robots, he explained that he went to the library to read books about outer space. It may not be necessary to add that young Arthur became quite an expert on space.

As for Mutant Ninja Turtles, 11-year-old Fedrik, by collecting and playing with the large Turtle family, learned about family connections that earlier had seemed a mystery to him. The Turtle family helped him to get a clear idea about the relationships between his parents, uncles and aunts, cousins, and grandparents.

How can a Barbie doll be used as a learning prop? One way is for interviewing older children about their toy play habits. Twelve-year-old girls explained to me that although they no longer played with their Barbie dolls, they used them as dress models in learning how to use a sewing machine.

It seems likely that as children grow older, they voluntarily use toys as learning props. If children's voluntary requests can be taken as indicators of their personal interests, an analysis of the content of 7- and 10-year-old children's letters to Santa Claus confirms a rather widespread assumption that children around the age of 10 are no longer interested in toys; nearly all of the 7-year-olds' requests, but only one-third of the 10-year-olds', were for toys (Almqvist, 1989a).

On the basis of systematic research as well as logic, it may finally be claimed that *educational toys* is a nonsense term. Rather, it seems plausible that any toy can be used to stimulate learning (if learning is the goal), provided that it is challenging to explore and that the child feels there is something worthwhile to learn from it. The following quotation summarizes this section:

The main point is that we have little compelling evidence of a connection between toys, all by themselves, and achievement, though such a connection is quite possible. What is more obvious is that, since the appearance of toys in the seventeenth century, we have steadily and progressively developed a belief that there is a connection between toys and achievement. It is a belief that has flourished more strongly with regard to the toys of the schoolroom (the so-called educational toys) than to the toys in the marketplace. But, increasingly in this century the distinction has been blurred as psychologists have emphasized the "information" potential of all objects and as toy manufacturers have continued, more effectively, their historical efforts to blot out the distinction between education and entertainment. So now it is taken for granted that most toys are educational in some respects. Many parents, however, are careful to keep the distinction alive between those toys they regard as mere baubles and those they regard as serving a child's achievement. (Sutton-Smith, 1986, p. 125)

Let's pretend

When you think of something and you want to do something but you don't have nothing so you pretend to do it. (Chaillé, 1978)[1]

To pretend, imagine, or make-believe obviously requires fantasy. One certainly needs fantasy to pretend that a tree branch is a rifle, a stone a potato, or a vacuum cleaner a fire-breathing dragon. There seems to be something in the shapes of things that makes it possible for children to accept the substitute for the real object. It is the "as if" that is so magical to children.

I am told often that children today do not fancy fantasy play as much as did an earlier generation. If this is true, it is pitiful,

[1]Chaillé conducted interviews with a group of 5- to 11-year-old children to illustrate children's conceptions of play and toys, as well as how children reason when they pretend. A 12-year-old boy's definition of a toy may illustrate the breadth of older children's fantasy: "A pen could be a toy if you built a house with it because you'd be using it as a toy. It could be a toy or a pen if you took it apart."

but I cannot help thinking that maybe the truth is that we adults just cannot see it because we are always so busy. Fantasy play does not require a whole ensemble or sweeping gestures but can occur on the inside, so to speak. "You could think it in your head and do the same realities and everything but still be another person" (Chaillé, 1978, p. 206).

Extrovert pretend play is, of course, easier to notice, especially when you are invited to take part in it. "Granny, let's pretend you are a mummy seal and I am your baby seal!" Six-year-old Erik made a "seal dive" into the swimming pool, yelling to "mummy seal" to come rescue her little baby seal. Which, of course, she did.

Play and reality – two different worlds

One early Sunday morning, an eel fishing party took place in our living room. Erik and his grandfather were sitting on a rug (the boat) on the floor (the sea) and had just caught a big eel (a rubber toy snake) with a fishing net (a crocheted woollen shawl). His grandmother, seated on a sofa close to the fishermen's "boat," turned to her husband to tell him something. She was immediately interrupted by Erik: "You can't talk to Grandpa now. We are far out on the sea fishing eel, and you are not with us."

For a moment, Erik the fisherman became Erik the boy, instructing an outsider about the boundaries between play and reality. It may be added that Grandma stayed quietly "on shore" until the two fishermen returned. The boundary between pretend play and reality is quite clear to the child. "Is it for real?" is a typical question when the child cannot hear the "play" tone in your voice. When you lean over the little baby and declare, "Now I am going to eat you up!", the baby howls with laughter, in spite of the macabre proposal. Of course, the baby has (luckily!) not understood a word of what you have just told him; he listened only to your voice, which (hopefully) used the play tone. The play tone is the opposite of the I-mean-business tone.

A summer game that is much esteemed by my 3-year-old grand-son Danilo is as follows: Securely equipped with swimming pads on his upper arms, he stands on the border of the swimming pool and shouts: "Look! I am going to jump in – SAY NO!". And the moment I yell "No, no, no!" in my most worried play tone, in he goes. The next second he comes up with a grin on his face, and we repeat the play over and over again. Danilo is playing "Let's pretend you forbid me to do it and I dare to do it anyway" and is assured by my play tone that I am pretending "Don't do it because I am worried that you'll drown." He is being himself all the time, just as I am being myself. The thrill is that we both act differently from the way we usually do.

Two rather opposed feelings are mixed in this type of pretend play: security in being oneself and excitement in acting contrary to oneself, in this case a naughty little boy and his worried grand-mother, a situation that would not be so funny if it was "for real." The "sense morale" of this story is that in telling the toddler what he or she is or is not allowed to do, your aspiration to make the toddler obey in other situations can fail if you for one second use your play tone instead of your firm I-mean-business tone.

Sutton-Smith has indeed put his finger on the heart of play when he explains that "Play is that sphere of differentiation and deviance which is the most universally available" (1986, p. 252). To do eel fishing on the living-room floor is the magic of "as if." It is exactly in harmony with Sutton-Smith's maxim that "In play, the significance of what is going on may come as much out of the minds of the players as out of the objects in their hands or the world to which those objects refer." The requisite in children's pretend play can be anything from nonrepresentational items to miniature cop-ies of real objects. As we saw in the play scene "naughty little boy jumps into the water," in which no toys were used (if you don't call a swimming pool a toy), real objects also can be used and allowed to represent exactly what they are. In the eel fishing play scene, however, a rug was a boat and a shawl was a fishing net. The only toy used was the rubber snake, which was awarded the role of an eel. Snake = eel. Shawl = fishing net. Once again, it may be presumed that it is the shape of an object that enables children to accept it as a substitute for the real thing.

Why bother about it?

The role of pretend play in the cognitive and social development of children has been of major theoretical interest to prominent scholars for decades (McLoyd, 1986). The hypotheses and theories about fantasy, its origin and functions, are diverse. Cognitive psychologists claim that fantasy is a creative cognitive skill associated with the ability to control impulses and to delay gratification. This is in contrast to psychoanalytic theory, which claims that fantasy chiefly serves as a neurotic defense and an outlet for unfulfilled wishes.

Why, then, are so many so anxious to find the secret behind fantasy? One reason may be the assumption that children with a high level of fantasy are equipped with many of the cognitive skills that contribute to creative functioning, which in turn leads to a richer, more productive adjustment to life. In the literature, such factors as originality, spontaneity, verbal fluency, free flow of ideas, and flexibility in adapting to new situations are all related to creativity (Pulaski, 1970).

If we agree to all this, there are still some questions to be answered if we are to help children develop such marvelous skills. Which is the chicken and which is the egg – fantasy or creativity? Are they two aspects of the same phenomenon? Dorothy and Jerome Singer (1990) suggest a distinction between imagination and creativity because "imagination seems freer and broader, since our thought may remain as private and as fanciful as we may want them to be, with no constraints" whereas creativity is manifest through products or actions. The Singers, in addition, suggest that "imagination, and earlier, the predisposition to pretend and make-believe play may well be necessary ingredients in stimulating and developing divergent thought." So it may be that creativity and imagination, or fantasy, are indeed two aspects of the same phenomenon.

The next question is: Which aspect was imprinted first? This question is crucial because if fantasy depends on cognitive skills, the fact that some children have poor fantasy may be due to cognitive deficiencies, and if fantasy can help to rectify such deficiencies, fantasy play training should be intensified. Peter Smith (1982, 1983) claims that "play tutoring can clearly boost fantasy play in those children who don't do very much of it," and that numerous studies have shown that "children who received fantasy play tutoring increased their social skills, language competence, cognitive abilities and creativity scores as well."

This is where the toys come in. It is well documented that mentally retarded children are poor pretend players and that toy play training is an excellent means of habilitation. Toys stimulate children's curiosity, but not all toys stimulate all children. This finding is the opposite of what the term *creative toys* seems to suggest.

A creative toy

The creative toy is a child of the 1970s, although its parents belong to the 1960s. Toys have been the core of debates ever since. What happened in those decades that caused all the fuss, which in turn created a veritable toy dilemma? For one thing, those were the decades of the baby boomers. They were also the decades when young mothers went to work outside the home and institutional child care came to be of crucial importance. The 1970s was the decade when feminist agitation was at a peak, and "the feminists also felt that the toy industry was exercising a sex-role stereotyping influence which they did not agree with" (Sutton-Smith, 1986, p. 172). Furthermore, the 1970s may be remembered as the "decade of equity," an ideology formed by the generation born in the 1940s. In the name of equity, and with the axiom that "one is as good as another," all children were "equalized" and supposed to be on the same – preferably high – level of fantasy. Children whose fantasy, in spite of this sacred belief, was poorer than other children's did not get much help. Templates were devastating because they would inhibit the children's "natural" fantasy, and many little ones sat struggling with their "innate" fantasy to create drawings and paintings, model clay, and so on. In line with the disapproval of templates and other gadgets as models in art making, toys, it was believed, should be ambiguous so that they could be interpreted by the children themselves to symbolize anything whatever. As a consequence of feminism campaigns (also called sexism), toys should also be unisex, so that they would not favor one gender (male) over the other (female). *Creative toys* came to be the privileged title for utterly plain, nonrepresentational items, sooner homemade than industrial, and well into the 1980s (if not today), nurseries were filled with leftovers like rolls of wallpaper, grocery boxes, and waste wood.

The logic behind the term *creative toys* is, no doubt, that all children are alike and that, therefore, the same toy will arouse the same response in all children. Children, however, are not all of a kind; each one has unique needs, abilities, and personality. Fantasy is not a ready-made package of one universal size.

What's in a toy that stimulates fantasy?

A common term in the research literature for nonrepresentational play materials is *low-realism toys*. Their opposites are, consequently, called *high-realism toys* and are typically miniature copies of real objects. Because the latter usually represent one thing only, it is often argued that they cannot be played with in more than one way and that they therefore hamper children's fantasy. The definition of a creative toy, then, would be "one that is malleable enough to represent anything." This reasoning, however, overlooks developmental factors; one obvious factor is that all children do not have the same level of fantasy or representational skills.

Investigators who examine the role of toys in children's pretend play seldom use the term *creative toys* but rather describe toys in terms of *structure, realism, richness* or *poorness of detail, similitude* and *verisimilitude,* which are often considered synonymous. I would like to point out one problem that arises when assuming that such terms are synonymous. For example, a toy rich in details is not necessarily high in realism. There is no doubt that, for example, My Little Pony is rich in details and that its shape is similar to that of a sturdy little horse. Still, it is not a very realistic horse. It is much smaller than the real thing, its body is hard, and it neither smells nor sounds like a real horse. In fact, as far as I know, it doesn't smell at all, nor does it neigh as a horse but is totally silent; but if it did make sounds it almost certainly would sound like a human being, as that is what it does in the children's program on television. Undoubtedly, realism is in the eye of the beholder.

Nevertheless, we may agree on the distinction between low-realism and high-realism toys; the former have less distinct counterparts in the real world, whereas the latter more or less exactly portray real objects. High-realism toys clearly represent real things and are therefore more familiar to young children. In addition, they are more likely to be used by adults when modeling pretend play, as joint adult–child pretend activities most often are centered on everyday objects that have strict functions (McLoyd, 1986).

It takes a great deal of fantasy to pretend that a baby doll can be fed and be spoken to, or to go out walking with or even be bitten by a stuffed textile toy animal, regardless of how realistic in features they both may be. In fact, there are such high-realism toys as cake-eating (!) and talking and crying baby dolls, and there are teddy bears with a beating heart and even teddy bears that answer to, or rather echo, what they are told. Although modern electronics make toys more and more like people, animals, cars, or trains in the real world, they are still far from the real stuff. The fact that children happily accept and manage to put life into them is a childhood miracle.

Prudence lenses and toy lenses

There is no evidence in the literature that children's play will be more diversified and nonstereotyped with low-structured playthings (Robinson & Jackson, 1987). Manufacturers of educational toys offered in preschool curriculum supply catalogs typically design such highly representational toys as wooden people, doll furniture, play villages, animals, cars, trucks, and trains to be low in realistic detail, with the implied intent of enhancing play elaboration and creativity. There is reason to reflect on the suggestion that "highly representational playthings are being designed with the pre-school teachers of upper-class parents in mind and not the children's interest" (Robinson & Jackson, 1987).

In considering the realism of a toy from the adult's perspective, the main question is how the child apprehends it. Toys have a certain function as well as a certain symbolism. Most often the function and the symbolism are mingled, which makes it – at least for the adult – difficult to understand the toy's magic. Earlier, I stressed the difference between the play tone and the "I mean business" tone. Here I would like to stress the difference between *toy lenses* and *prudence lenses*. When you put on your prudence lenses, you regard the toy from an adult perspective only and – with all respect for your wisdom – fail to see the magic of it. Only by changing to toy lenses will you be able to see the toy from the child's perspective.

Take, for example, the so-called trendy toys, which, not unlike magnets, draw children to them. Most adults find them stereotypic and – not seldom – violent in appearance. The earlier-mentioned Mutant Ninja Turtle is, to my eyes, a grotesque, menacing-looking mixture of animal and human being; whatever can one do with it?

However, the way my grandson Erik played with it changed my mind, at least where the play repertoire is concerned. First, the Turtle was a parachute jumper who "accidentally" crashed into the big sea. The parachute was a little party hat with a rubber band tied under the arms or the Turtle, and the sea was the kitchen sink filled with water. Later, I met the Turtle in the shape of a web-footed frogman (with paper "webs" taped under his feet) and also in the role of Batman "flying" around the room with his (paper) cape on, rescuing everyone worthy of that brave enterprise. As the Turtle symbolizes both an animal and a human being, from a child's perspective its magic is that it can be given either role. Maybe it is this mixture of human and animal qualities that makes children find toys like the forest family and My Little Pony so appealing. We cannot, however, give the toy all the credit for an extensive play repertoire. It takes fantasy too.

High- and low-fantasy children and toys

Although the general assumption is that children are filled with fantasy, it cannot be taken for granted that all children have the same degree of this gift. Some children find it difficult to pretend, whereas others pretend easily about almost everything. A typical assumption in studies of the meaning of toy structure in children's pretend play is that high-fantasy children fruitfully use low-realism toys in their pretend play and that low-fantasy children need high-realism toys to take the step into fantasy land. Therefore, in studies of children's pretend play, not only are the toys divided into high- and low-realism categories, but the subjects are divided into high-fantasy and low-fantasy children.

A number of studies of how structure and children's fantasy or pretend play interact indicate that low-realism toys typically elicit a greater variety of themes than high-realism toys. On the other hand, it has been suggested that low-realism toys may increase constructional play on behalf of fantasy play, whereas high-realism toys increase fantasy play on behalf of constructional play (Nakamine, 1979). It might thus be tempting to take one or the other side, decide which kind of play is preferable for the child's development, and then support the child with the "right" toys. Such decisions, however, are totally pointless. The "best" play is the play the child prefers, and the "best" toys are those that the child finds pleasure in. Children do not say "Now I'll improve my thinking by means of constructional play" or "Now I'll play something that can develop my creativity." They just play, and usually they do not do one instead of the other. Rather, they say, "Let's take all the blocks and pretend we build the highest house in the world."

High-fantasy children typically express greater interest and delight in toys and generally respond more strongly to low-realism than to high-realism toys, whereas low-fantasy children seem to prefer the latter. Furthermore, boys typically exhibit greater enjoyment in their fantasy play, as well as more activity, than do girls. Girls, however, are usually more liberal in their attitudes toward opposite-gender toys than boys are. As one investigator remarks: "While the girls gave admiring remarks about the boys' toys, the boys showed their contempt about girls' toys by statements such as: All girls' things...nothing I like" (Pulaski, 1970, p. 535).

In summary, findings indicate that a variety of factors is involved in children's responses to toys, including age, gender, and level of fantasy. However, the methods as well as the findings of these studies are diverse, not only because investigators have different ideas about toy realism, but also because children and adults comprehend realism differently. Ultimately, it is what is in the mind of the child that is worth our efforts to discover.

I conclude by quoting Brian Sutton-Smith, who gives this illustration of the creative toy dilemma:

> The odd outcome with toys is that there is the pervasive stereotype that if children are playing with boxes or blocks or malleable materials which are not already images of something else, then they are imagining; but if they are playing with realistic toys, they are not imagining. So public opinion is divided about toys. Some are regarded as vehicles for the imagination and some are regarded as cramps to the same process. (1986, p. 228)

4
The war play debate

PETER K. SMITH

The debate about war toys, though not new, has taken on new life over the last decade. The deregulation of television in the United States in the 1980s, the loosening of restrictions in the United Kingdom, and the coming of satellite and cable television, together with the development of program-length commercials and the associated marketing of war toys, have reawakened fears of many parents and teachers about this kind of play. A similar debate in the 1960s (the Vietnam War period in the United States) was documented by Andreas (1969). Advertisements for modern war toys in the magazines *Toys and Novelties* and *Sears Christmas Book* nearly tripled over the period 1961–64/5. Andreas claimed that this was an anticipation of demand rather than a response to it, and that following protests by parents and educators, advertising fell to earlier levels by 1967.

The more recent wave of concern has provoked two books by Nancy Carlsson-Paige and Diane Levin. In the first book, *The War Play Dilemma: Balancing Needs and Values in the Early Childhood Classroom* (1987), they contrast the developmental view that play, including war play, is a primary vehicle through which children work on developmental issues, with the sociopolitical view that children learn militaristic political concepts and values through war play. They advocate that teachers and parents, rather than banning war play, should intervene to channel it into more educational and acceptable forms. Their second book, a more practical handbook entitled *Who's Calling the Shots? How to Respond Effectively to Children's Fascination with War Play and War Toys* (1990), develops this advice more fully.

The developmental viewpoint, as they characterize it, is that war play is a natural kind of play; that children have always enjoyed play fighting and toy soldiers; and that modern war toys are just an extension of this tendency. War play is seen as clearly pretend; as one boy who wanted a toy gun responded to his father's abhorrence of violence, "But Dad, I don't want to shoot anybody, I just want to play" (*Boston Globe,* March 1990). Furthermore, it is argued that war play does no more than reflect aspects of the adult world and help the child come to terms with it. At its strongest, supporters of war play argue that it may serve cathartic functions and/or help children cope with issues of good and evil. At least, it is argued that adults should interfere minimally with what are and should be activities that children freely choose for themselves (see also Sutton-Smith, 1988; Sutton-Smith, Gerstmyer & Meckley, 1988).

Opponents of war play argue that such forms of play impoverish the child's imagination and encourage aggressive behavior. As with the objections to violent television programs, many such critics argue that the distinction between pretense and reality is not absolute, and that the steady incorporation of war toys and violence into play scripts may in fact make violent behavior more common later. A critique somewhat independent of this one is that war play exemplifies the worst aspect of a consumerist society. Children are encouraged to buy toys that not only promote violent play, but also play that is stereotyped and repetitive in its continual enactment of simple good-versus-evil scenarios (Carlsson-Paige & Levin, 1987). Teachers, especially nursery school and kindergarten teachers, often ban war toys for these reasons (U.S.: Sutton-Smith et al., 1988; Germany: Wegener-Spöhring, 1989a; this is also the case in other Western European countries, including the U.K.).

The debate has also spawned many media articles, with headlines such as "Shooting Times" and "Gun Law for the Young"

(*The Guardian,* November 1988) and "The Experts Disagree on the Issue of Children and War Toys" (*Boston Globe,* March 1990). There is clearly concern and disagreement about the issues; and the disagreement, as well as reflecting different perspectives and values, reveals a lack of sound knowledge, good research, and clear thinking in this area.

In this chapter, I hope to do two things: first, to summarize some recent research we have carried out on attitudes of parents in England and in Italy to war toys and to demonstrate the variety of viewpoints they hold; and second, to suggest some conceptual issues that future researchers and thinkers should consider if we are to make real progress in this debate.

Parents' attitudes toward war play

Although it is clear from media articles, and from the books by Carlsson-Paige and Levin, that parents differ considerably in their attitudes toward war play, there has been little systematic research on this issue. Recently, I and some colleagues obtained data from 84 parents in Sheffield, England, and from 316 parents in Bologna and Cosenza, Italy, where similar concerns about war toys have been emerging (Costabile, Genta, Zucchini, Smith & Harker, 1992).

We adapted and extended a questionnaire used by Carlsson-Paige and Levin (1987), which defined war play as "forms of combat play including

(i) play with imitation or pretend weapons (e.g., guns, swords)
(ii) play with combat figures such as Superhero, Action, Star Wars or Transformer toys
(iii) acting out a combat role such as Rambo, GI Joe, He-Man,"

and followed this with a series of questions about the kinds of war play their children engaged in, the response of the parents, and their attitude toward war play and some other activities. The questionnaire was used in England in late 1989–early 1990, and, translated and used in Italy in late 1990–early 1991. Most of the respondents were mothers, and their children were generally aged 3 to 6 years.

Our main findings were as follows:

*There is a strong gender difference in both countries, with a majority of boys but only a small minority of girls reported to engage in war play. (Similar findings are reported in Germany by Wegener-Spöhring, 1989a, based on interviews with children, and in the United States by Watson and Peng, 1992, based on parent questionnaires.) For many children the frequency of war play was only about once a week, but for some boys it was observed on most days.

*The most common form of war play described was weapon play:

- "makes swords and guns from cardboard boxes and generally leaps around brandishing them";
- "pretends to shoot people with a toy gun. Says 'hands up' then shoots";

followed by playing with combat figures:

- "plays battles with toy soldiers and weapons";
- "Star Wars/Transformer toys used to act out an invented story involving quest of some kind with adversaries to be overcome, not necessarily by killing but can be";

and acting out a combat role:

- "pretends to be He-Man or a Ghostbuster";
- "character leader in Thundercats 'Lion O'."

*Parents reported that those children who did engage in war play generally started at 2 or 3 years of age and were influenced by television, peers, and older siblings. The parents of those children who did not engage in war play mostly reported a general lack of interest by the child (rather than parental discouragement per se as the reason, though this did sometimes occur).

*Most children were reported to enjoy rough-and-tumble play. This included tickling games, chase and catch, pillow fights, wrestling, and use of pretend themes such as lions and monsters.

*Views of parents on how to react to war play fell into three categories:

(a) Discourage:
   - "I do not buy any toys in this field as I feel it makes children very aggressive";
   - "try to discourage him; make him play other games";
   - "I say it is very noisy and does she really want to kill people because that is what happens when people are shot. As soon as she puts the toy down I remove it."

(b) Allow the play within limits:
   - "If only occasionally I would ignore it. But if more regular I would offer a change of activity";
   - "I'm bothered if it's excessively noisy and violent and frequent but otherwise can accept it as part of a child's acting out internal tensions and external experiences";
   - "if the play involves other children who are overzealous in their play I put a stop to it. If it is just fun with a friend I do not mind."

(c) Allow unconditionally:
   - "It is just imaginative play that all children need. It helps to get rid of frustration which has built up in them";
   - "harmless, like adults reading war books, watching war films. It is a fact of life that conflict exists and a child learns all things through play";
   - "I sometimes get involved."

We found a fairly even spread of responses across these three categories. The Discourage response was considerably more frequent among parents whose children were reported not to engage in war play, whether these were boys or girls.

*The majority of parents (about three-quarters) thought that children should not be allowed to bring war toys into a nursery, play group, or first school, regardless of whether their own child did or did not play with war toys at home. Over half of the parents thought that the best response of play-group supervisors or teachers to war play, if it occurs, is to try to turn it to more constructive ends (rather than prevent it, or allow it like any other kind of play).

*A cluster analysis of attitude items contrasted parents favorable to all kinds of play (and permissive of violent TV programs) and those not so favorable or permissive. In the Italian sample, a particularly strong central cluster depicted parents with favorable attitudes toward war play, rough-and-tumble play, and buying toy weapons and combat figures compared to those with unfavorable attitudes to all of these activities. For the English sample, two separate clusters were obtained. The first contained items relating to attitudes toward war play and violent TV, and toward the child's often engaging in war play, with a particularly strong link between attitudes toward war play and buying toy weapons and combat figures. The second cluster linked attitudes toward pretend play and rough-and-tumble play. Italian parents linked rough-and-tumble play strongly with war play and toy weapons, whereas English parents did not.

Parental attitudes toward war play in the home are clearly diverse. Some parents strongly discourage war play and would never buy toy weapons or combat figures; some are uncertain; some think it natural and, indeed, may actually join in. Many parents did comment about the dilemma they often faced in dealing with their children's wishes on the matter.

Watching certain TV programs may encourage children both to urge their parents to get the associated toy products and to act out the associated themes; most reported war play does involve combat figures and toy weapons, and these are often produced and marketed in close connection with particular children's programs or cartoon series (Kline & Pentecost, 1990). Peer pressure has also been reported by parents, and it is clear that war play may "run in families" to some extent, as we found it to be more likely when older siblings also did it.

The attitudes of most parents in our sample supported the ban on such toys imposed in many European nursery and infant schools. Perhaps parents who may be equivocal about banning such play at home may feel that school should foster a more educational environment and that the ethos of noninterference in children's play has less relevance in this setting. If war play does occur in school, there is again some parental consensus that the best policy is not to stop it entirely but to turn it to more constructive ends, as advocated by Carlsson-Paige and Levin (1987, 1990). Banning all forms of war play seems futile (because children will do it furtively), possibly counterproductive (because of the prevalence of war themes in the wider society), and an unnecessary infringement of the principle that children should have reasonable freedom to play as they desire.

It is unlikely that any consensus can be reached about the actions of parents in the home. Parents vary greatly in their attitudes here; and in the absence of much better research evidence on the effects of war play, it would appear premature to do more than point out to interested parents the different perspectives on the issues and, possibly, the results of relevant research. It is to a further examination of the research that I now turn.

Issues in studying the effects of war toys

Compared to research on the effects of TV violence, which has been extensive even if still inconclusive, research on war toys has been scanty. However, a number of studies have, for example, examined the kinds of play children do with different sorts of toys (including war toys), the kinds of play and social interaction children do after playing with different kinds of toys (including war toys), and the correlates of playing with war toys. Sutton-Smith (1988) and Goldstein (1992) have reviewed the relevant studies to date and have cogently pointed out that all were flawed in various respects. Taking these critiques as a starting point, I summarize some of the main issues that I feel future research should grapple with if we are to make further progress. These include:

- What we mean by war play.
- How we measure the outcomes of war play.
- What process measures we include.
- How studies are designed.
- How we evaluate the results of studies.

What we mean by war play

It is clear that war play is not real aggression, which can itself take a variety of forms (physical and verbal, direct and indirect, instrumental and hostile). Play, unlike real aggression, is generally enjoyable for the participants.

War play should also be distinguished from rough-and-tumble play or play fighting. Rough-and-tumble play involves chasing and fleeing, mock wrestling, grappling, tumbling, kicking, and so on, done without the intent to hurt the play partner. Parents often do it with young children, and it is a common activity among children throughout the school years. Although some psychologists have confused play fighting and real fighting, research has shown that children can tell them apart from an early age, and by around 8 years of age can describe many of the cues used to distinguish them (Smith, Hunter, Carvalho & Costabile, 1992). Rarely does play fighting turn into real fighting.

Although the developmental function of rough-and-tumble play remains partly obscure, it seems that many children enjoy it, that it is often done with friends, and that besides developing physical skills, this play has a role in social bonding (Smith, 1989). In my view, we know enough about rough-and-tumble play to suggest that, in its normal forms, there is no reason generally to discourage it in the home or school and, indeed, some reasons to encourage it as not only enjoyable but also useful in development.

Although much rough-and-tumble is adequately described in terms of the straight physical actions of wrestling, chasing, and so on, some of it involves clear pretend or sociodramatic components. Children may pretend to be spacemen, monsters, witches, and so forth, incorporating rough-and-tumble behaviors in their game.

This kind of play is, again, common; and generally, play theorists have seen some benefits to sociodramatic play in terms of understanding social roles, developing verbal skills, and perspective taking (Smilansky, 1968). Even if some of these claims are exaggerated, it would be going against the grain of most research to say that most of these games had harmful effects.

The types of war play identified by Carlsson-Paige and Levin (1987), and recognized by parents in our own survey, center on the use of toy weapons, use of combat figures, and acting out superhero roles. These could be argued to be distinguishable from most common forms of rough-and-tumble play (and did seem to be distinguished at least by the English parents in our own survey). Some war play, especially superhero role play, may incorporate some rough-and-tumble in it, but the distinguishing feature of war play seems to be pretend aggression using objects (weapons) or with objects (combat figures). The superhero role play often involves these objects; if it did not, it would probably not seem objectionable to parents.

Beresin (1989) has suggested that it may be useful to distinguish *fantastic* from *realistic* objects, and perhaps we may further separate out *traditional* ones. Traditional objects would be weapons such as swords, shields, bows and arrows, and figures/roles such as Robin Hood, cowboys, and Indians. Although realistic, these are generally well removed historically from contemporary experience. Fantastic objects would be weapons such as light sabers and figures/roles such as He-Man, Darth Vader, and Ninja Turtles embedded in contemporary experience of a nonrealistic kind. Realistic objects would be imitation guns and bombs and figures/

roles such as Rambo, GI Joe, or participants in contemporary conflicts (e.g., Serbs and Croats, Americans and Iraqis). Given the clear understanding children have of the pretend–real distinction from about 4 years of age on (Flavell, Flavell & Green, 1987), it would appear to be more difficult to argue that traditional or fantastic kinds of war play are more likely than realistic war play to lead to later militaristic views.

Finally, it should be clear whether the child is directing pretend aggression to a toy or to another child. Making two toy soldiers pretend to fight each other (which is, after all, what they are designed for and what soldiers actually do) may be worth distinguishing from pretending to shoot another child. This distinction can nevertheless become difficult in interactive video games, in which a child may be shooting at a pretend person moving on the screen.

How we measure the outcomes of war play

Perhaps the most prominent shortcoming of earlier studies on the effects of playing with war toys has been the lack of sophistication in outcome measures. Generally, studies looked at aggression, sometimes confusing the three types of behavior we have just distinguished – real aggression, rough-and-tumble play (seldom categorized separately until recently), and pretend aggression (often labeled *thematic aggression*). Clearly, these different kinds of activities must be assessed separately.

This may not always be easy in practice. In some exploratory work carried out by Little (1989), we observed the kinds of play that children engaged in with (1) TV war toys (He-Man, Lion-O, Skeletor, Tongue-Lash, Transformers), (2) non-TV war toys (a fort, toy knights, tanks, action men), and (3) neutral toys (farm yard, animals, tractor, digger, cars). The study was done with 24 children (15 boys, 9 girls) aged 3 to 4½ years in a play group which (unusually) did not ban war toys. The three sets of toys were available on a large table in one room for half-hour sessions on 5 successive days. Each session was filmed.

We found that although boys played with all of these toys more than girls did, children of both genders played with the TV war toys most often and with the neutral toys least; often, possibly an effect of novelty/familiarity. When playing with any of the toy sets, pretend aggression was much more frequent than real aggression. Pretend aggression was more frequent with both sets of war toys than with the neutral toys, not surprisingly; we scored pretend aggression when actions such as fighting, hitting, shooting, and so on were accompanied by positive (smiling, laughing) or neutral facial expressions. Real aggression did not differ significantly among the three sets of toys; here we scored such incidents when accompanied by negative facial expressions. Even then, most of this real aggression was directed by a child to a toy or by the child causing a toy to attack another toy (e.g., getting one figure to attack another one while snarling or with an angry face). Only a very small proportion of this aggression (about 7%) was child–child, that is, clearly aggressive in terms of usual definitions of the term.

Another issue is the complexity of play sequences. Carlsson-Paige and Levin (1987) claim that much war play, especially that influenced by recent TV programming, is repetitive, stereotyped, and impoverished in its content and format, slavishly following simple screen-fed scenarios of good and evil, battle and destruction (hence their suggestions for constructive intervention in this play when it occurs). Yet, this allegation is little documented. More complex play may be more interesting and developmentally challenging and useful for a child, but a lot of play, of whatever kind, is repetitive. Is war play more so than other kinds?

Short-term and long-term outcomes also need to be distinguished. So far, studies have concentrated almost exclusively on short-term outcomes – what the child does while playing with war toys or soon afterward. Yet many of the worries of war toy opponents are about long-term outcomes – such as militaristic views in adulthood or the increased likelihood of the violent use of guns.

We should bear in mind two aspects of this view; one is a direct effect of individual experience – that permitting violent play with guns leads to later tolerance of gun use in that individual, for example; the other is a more general view of social norms – that permitting or encouraging gun play and war play generally will help create and maintain a society in which the level of violence is high.

What process measures we include

We need to look closely at the amount of war play that children actually engage in. In our survey, many children were reported to engage in war play once a week or less. Does this frequency result in any lasting impact? Adults who drink a great deal of alcohol may suffer adverse consequences, but one drink a day has been argued on recent evidence to be beneficial. Similarly, there may be threshold effects for any lasting consequences of war play. Perhaps a small amount actually has beneficial developmental effects, whereas a large amount is cause for concern. But as yet, we do not know. Straightforward linear correlations with frequency are unlikely to reveal such curvilinear effects, if they exist.

We need to pay more attention to individual differences. We have already noted a pervasive gender difference in frequency of war play. However, another consideration is that war play may have different effects on different children. Relevant aspects here might be temperament, security of attachment and internal working models of relationships, and sociometric status with peers. For example, some of the research on watching violent TV suggests little harmful effect except for a minority of children with disturbed views of relationships who may, indeed, adopt some violent scripts from TV viewing. As another example, Pellegrini (1988) has found that for most children rough-and-tumble play is quite harmless, but for sociometrically rejected children there is an enhanced probability that it will turn into real fighting. Similarly, we may find that war toy play is harmless for the majority of children but that it may feed into the more disturbed needs of some children who view relationships in more violent or hostile terms than most.

Another important factor is parental mediation. We have seen the variety of parental responses to war play. It may be an important influence on how it affects children, and not necessarily in obvious ways. One English mother wrote that "there is a ban on war toys in our house...it's a straightforward rule, which my six-year-old son understands...he knows that real guns maim and kill and that his parents dislike representations of them in any form." However, this mother also laments that he "finds them fascinating, exciting and desirable and is now so gun conscious that his eyesight has apparently developed a superhuman capacity for spotting weapons at a range of several hundred metres...it has stimulated the development of his cunning to an almost admirable degree" (Greenwell, 1988). As others have pointed out, too rigid a ban may be counterproductive.

How studies are designed

In trying to design research studies, there are all the obvious considerations of issues such as sample size and reliability of measures, as well as issues about definitions of war play and the range of outcome measures, as just discussed. In addition, there are issues to do with experimenter bias. There is the danger of experimenters looking for and finding what they want to find. This has been true in studies of play generally (Smith, 1988) and of studies of TV violence, and Sutton-Smith (1988) has pointed out the similar dangers in studies of war toys.

There is also a continuing tension between experimental and correlational studies. The experimental studies in this domain have generally involved small samples, looking at very short-term effects, and open to accusations of experimenter effects (Sutton-Smith, 1988). Yet, they do at least purport to identify cause–effect relationships.

A recent study by Watson and Peng (1992) improves on a number of previous studies. It clearly separates real aggression, pretend aggression, and rough-and-tumble play and looks at several process measures (including parental attitudes) and outcome measures. These authors did find – for boys (not for girls) – an association between a history of toy gun play and levels of real aggression in 3- to 5-year-olds in a day care center. However, the study is correlational. This means that we do not know that the gun play has helped to cause the aggression; it may even be simply that children who are more aggressive – because of temperament, parental rearing strategies, or other reasons – enjoy playing with toy guns more than other children.

Methodological shortcomings, unfortunately, are found in any study. The history of research on the effects of TV violence is sobering in this regard. After several decades of research and a large number of studies, the effects of watching violent TV on children's development is still a matter of controversy (Freedman, 1986; Friedrich-Cofer & Huston, 1986). Nevertheless, we can hope to move toward a more informed picture if enough studies accumulate that avoid some of the most basic errors mentioned.

How we evaluate the results of studies

Even if we were to get a clear picture of the effects of TV violence on children from future studies, we may still argue about what action this information might imply. Judgments about action depend on values. Beresin (1989) points out that although many people oppose gun use and interpersonal violence, this attitude is by no means unanimous. Many other people are in favor of guns and justify using violence for political or even personal ends.

Suppose, however, a democratic society in which the predominant belief is that, wherever possible, disputes should be settled by nonviolent means. Further suppose that – unlike Northern Ireland, for example, or the former Yugoslavia – most people believe this most of the time.

Now consider the various needs and desires of differing persons in the war toys debate. We can consider children themselves, their parents, teachers, and toy manufacturers, for example.

As a first approximation, we may assume that children tend to play in ways that satisfy their own needs. As the British Toy and Hobby Manufacturers Association put it, "children tend to play with those toys that meet their current social, physical and psychological needs." This conclusion is true and will be in the children's own interests – provided that their perceptions of needs are not greatly distorted by external pressures. Such pressures might come from parents, teachers, or TV advertising, for example. Some children may internalize strongly held parental wishes and beliefs. Some may be persuaded to want a toy because it is promoted as something exciting that all children want. Some advocates of children's freedom of play from intervention by teachers or parents do not always show similar concern for their freedom from media manipulation.

The interests of a particular child may not always coincide with those of others. A child may possibly need some violent play because it helps to develop social skills involving violence or coping with violence, manipulation of others, and dominance. One could argue that all children need these skills to some extent (perhaps boys more than girls if males generally experience more competition than females). It is to the advantage of any child to know how to hold his or her own in a world that – even in peaceful societies – has some violence. We may want a peaceful world in general, but we should be aware that we may be sacrificing children's own interests for wider and somewhat remote goals if we totally forbid them war toys.

A disturbed child may need to develop skills of manipulation and violence to a greater extent than most children. Research shows that some children consistently follow a developmental path of high aggression (Patterson, DeBaryshe & Ramsey, 1989). Such children may need and choose violent toys, but we should be aware that using such a justification may further the development of antisocial behavior and criminality.

Parents are likely to have their children's interests in mind but may misinterpret or distort them; in addition, they have their own sets of interests. They may find war play upsetting because of the memories it triggers of violence they themselves have experienced – in the Vietnam War, for example. Or they may just dislike the noisiness and intrusiveness of war play or the financial demands of children asking for new superhero toys.

Teachers are likely to represent the values of the 'ideal society' of middle-class, educated people; and indeed, opposition to war toys seems particularly concentrated in the teaching profession. Irrespective perhaps of children's own needs, many teachers may see part of their role as being to try, through educating tomorrow's citizens, to bring about a more peaceful and democratic social climate and future society. Banning war toys can be seen as a response to this desire and can be defended as such, but it should not be confused with children's own needs per se.

Toy manufacturers have their own agenda. They are primarily after profit. They may sometimes also bear in mind their reputation for good taste and the reactions of consumers. These latter points were clearly stated in an editorial in the U.S. trade journal *Toys and Novelties* in 1966: "Far too little thought is given by toy men to values and taste . . . what is required is that much deeper and much more searching consideration be given to the values inherent in the toys they produce and sell" (quoted in Andreas, 1969). Some toy manufacturers, such as Lego, have avoided marketing toys with obviously warlike features. However, other manufacturers clearly follow the line of one store buyer: "our business is to give people what they want, and they'll want TV toys. It's as simple as that." This is a frank admission that the values of toy manufacturers need not coincide with the real needs of children or parents.

Conclusions

Where does this leave us? Personally, and in our present state of knowledge, I find little to support the extreme anti–war-toy position of some parents who ban any kind of war play in their home. They have the right to do it, but I suspect it is unnecessary and counterproductive. As a parent, I would be worried only if my child was obsessed with war toys or with violence in his or her play; I would then seek the reasons for this attitude, probably outside the toys themselves.

Some ban on realistic war toys in nurseries and first schools may be reasonable. Schools have an explicit educational agenda and cater to a wide variety of children. Given these facts and the controversial nature of the issue, it is probably better to risk a small infringement of children's liberty than to antagonize a substantial number of parents and possibly risk feeding the aggressive fantasies of a few disturbed children. However, it seems counterproductive to carry bans to extreme lengths (such as forbidding making guns with Lego).

Toy manufacturers, stores, and TV companies surely have a responsibility along with their powers of persuasion and advertising. Taking refuge in simple slogans about giving people what they want when wants can be socially manipulated is double-talk. However, parents cannot rely on all toy companies to show responsibility voluntarily. Either legal restraints or strong public pressure are likely to be needed. Relevant issues are the power of modern advertising methods and the ability of children to understand the nature of advertising, as well as the nature of some products. Some advertisements have been found to be sufficiently sophisticated that only by around 12 years of age do children begin to understand their commercial intent (Young, 1991). Sometimes advertising in the accepted sense of "drawing attention to" seems to turn into elaborate forms of deception and manipulation (Kline & Pentecost, 1990). Also, some products are clearly offensive. As the *Toys and Novelties* editorial cited earlier put it, "a game based on the Ku Klux Klan, for example ... or ... a miniature Nazi concentration camp complete with crematoriums for turning tiny figures of Jews into soap ... obviously go far beyond the bounds of good taste ... no matter how well they might sell ... it is my personal opinion that there are toy items currently being produced which transgress just as far" (quoted in Andreas, 1969). Today, almost 25 years later, there are other games available – such as interactive videos in which Arab or black figures are shot at – that are certainly subject to such criticism in terms of perpetuating ethnic stereotypes. There surely are some toys, and some ways of selling toys, that are not acceptable to most people, whatever the eventual verdict of research evidence on the more usual forms of war play turns out to be.

5

War toys and aggressive play scenes

GISELA WEGENER-SPÖHRING

Introductory play scene

I begin by reporting a play scene. The participants were children 5 years of age in a kindergarten.

Rickeracke, rickeracke: rockets, crocodile, and saw

Three children are in the process of building spaceships and rockets, they say, out of Lego blocks. Martin flies his rocket against his head and simultaneously makes flying sounds: "Ui, ui; oo-pf, oo-pf"; he then makes sounds like a German ambulance siren: "Tatoo-tata, tatoo-tata."

Martin: "I have an extinguisher rocket" and makes motor sounds, "Humm, humm, neeh."

Anja: "The rockets can only fly this way." She demonstrates this with her hand and simultaneously makes loud noises, "Teeha eeha, teeha eeha. My rocket can turn."

Bernd: "I have a spaceship. Fire!! Crack, boing, boing" (loud sounds, with a great deal of playful emphasis).

Martin: (Flies his rocket in Anja's direction) "You'd better watch out that it doesn't smash your rocket."

Anja: "I have a crocodile."

Martin: "I'm going to hit you one on your head. I'm taking my axe with me."

Bernd: "I'm taking my metal saw and: rickeracke, rickeracke."

Anja: "Yesterday there was the show with the mouse" (a television program).

Bernd: (Sings) "Spaceship, spaceship, once upon a time Lila, lula, once upon a time."

The children have chosen a warlike theme that they play harmoniously and dynamically. They are very imaginative: Rockets can fly against one's head, this way or that, and make one sound or the other; they can extinguish fires and turn as well. A spaceship opens fire. At this point their play escalates into a very aggressive sequence, which nonetheless remains play and in which the children are equally matched playmates. Anja counters Martin's threat to smash her rocket with a symbol of strength, the crocodile. If the boys then think up the axe and saw as a further intensification, the final "rickeracke, rickeracke" (imitating the sound made by a saw) goes almost too far. A further intensification of that play, which is aggressive, frightening, and threatening, would probably overtax the children and disrupt their play. Anja, however, restores the balance in their play with élan by reducing tension referring to that which is trusted and familiar: the program with the mouse. The boys can accept this mitigation; play is play, play is let's pretend: "Once upon a time, lila, lula, once upon a time." The play sequence ends with Bernd's singsong, to the satisfaction of all.

It is evident "that children are radically competent in their play" (Sutton-Smith & Magee, 1989). It is also evident, on the other hand, that play follows special dynamics, a specific dramaturgy of which we are hardly aware. Our objective was to research these dynamics and this dramaturgy, to understand, but not to regulate them. Aggression in play, which I focus on in accordance with my topic, was only one aspect of this research.

The concept of aggression

It is not my intention to present a survey of definitions, theories, and research. This information can be obtained in two recent publications of the British Toy and Hobby Association (Goldstein, 1988; Jukes, 1991). In addition, Sutton-Smith (1988) has written a comprehensive survey of research. I also do not wish to entangle myself in the theoretical dispute of psychologists that goes so far as to demand the abolishment of the concept of aggression (Mummendey, 1983). The definitions promulgated there are of limited use here because they begin with the injurious or harmful intention of the aggressor: "Aggression is any form of behavior directed toward the goal of harming or injuring another living being who is motivated to avoid such treatment" (Baron, 1977).

The definitions of Goldstein (1988, p. 19) and Jukes (1991, p. 4) are similar. I have problems with these definitions when I attempt to describe playful aggression. With respect to our research, the distinction between *play-immanent* (i.e., remaining at the "let's pretend" level) and *play-external* (i.e., occurring at the level of reality) is of central importance. The two are completely different, and I do not want to be found guilty of the "sin," as Sutton-Smith (1988) termed it, of confusing them. I therefore describe aggression pragmatically in terms of the following behaviors:

Verbal
  – Telling off, abusing, screaming at another child
  – Threatening
  – Speaking ill of another child/of the product of another child

- Speaking pejoratively
- Ridicule

Physical
- Kicking, hitting, pinching, shoving
- Aggressive gestures (e.g., balling the fists, flicking the bird)

Object directed
- Taking something away from another child, break something
- Aggression directed at things that belong to another child
- Aggression directed at things/nondirected aggression
- Aggression directed at one's own person

Play-immanent aggression, play fighting, and rough-and-tumble play are usually associated with physical movement (running, leaping, wrestling, and shoving) and many loud noises (onomatopoeic vocalizations, calling, and screaming). Yet there are also quieter forms (e.g., "Cäsar im Schrank" [Caesar in the Closet]); Wegener-Spöhring, 1989a,c). It is clear that play-immanent aggression is always accompanied by positive emotions; that the participants hit one another only by using their open hands (not their fists); and that the exchanging of roles between victor and loser, aggressor and victim, pursuer and pursued is particularly important. "Rough-and-tumble play is an enjoyable set of behaviors" (Pellegrini, 1987). Of course, it is often not easy to distinguish play-immanent from play-external aggression. Children, however, says Sutton-Smith, "make those distinctions fairly easily and rather early in their own lives" (1988, p. 64). This seems plausible. We therefore did not construct any tests; rather, we let children themselves speak on the topic of war toys, and in a second project we observed their (aggressive) play scenes for hours. We wanted to learn about and understand the strange world of children's play. (By "we" I mean my assistants, Sigrun Hafa and Anke Jagels, and me.)

Significance of war toys

We developed a format for a structured group discussion and a short questionnaire. Then we went to the schools. Class discussions were held in 20 fourth-grades in Göttingen, Herzberg/Harz, and Bremerhaven in 1984. The complete data cover 429 children, most of them 10 years old (218 boys, 211 girls). One class did not fill out the questionnaire, so there are discussion data for an additional 30 children. The discussions were led and evaluated by the three of us.

We told the children that we wanted to talk with them about "toys one can fight with." The discussions all followed the same pattern. We gave a brief introduction, asked a lead-in question followed by nine questions for discussion, and then formulated a final statement. Afterward the pupils completed a questionnaire with eight questions. The time allotted was one class period (45 min). We also tried to interview the teachers briefly at the end of each session, but this was not always possible.

We collected 681 different remarks on the subject "toys one can fight with" and assigned each of these to one of nine categories. This categorizing was always done by two of us (see Wegener-Spöhring, 1985, 1986).

The situation in the schools

Our project was influenced by three different groups: local authorities, teachers, and children. We first had to contact the local authorities in order to get official permission for the project. They were reserved: "So much research has already been done. Lessons are too often being disrupted." Resistance was so great that we were not able to obtain permission to enter schools in Göttingen. It was obvious that we were dealing with a delicate subject. We had no choice but to go to other towns outside of Göttingen.

The teachers who know us were frank; the others were quite

cautious. This was indeed a delicate subject, but not only for the authorities. "We have already dealt with these things," some said immediately. Some apologized for not having spoken about war toys yet. Some said nothing at all. Of course, they were just as unsure as we were. What should one do: forbid, ignore, or tolerate war toys? There was the suspicious eye of the authorities as well as the potential criticism of parents looming over them. I can well understand the teachers' uncertainty.

The children were enthusiastic. It was no problem for them to talk about this topic for 35 minutes; on the contrary, they would have liked to talk much longer. The discussions were intense and vacillated between being fun and earnest, noisy and quiet, boisterous and embarrassing. It was obvious that nobody had ever asked them about such an important thing in their lives. They told us many things, with a frankness and a reckless abandon that were almost shocking. They revealed their intimate and secret play world even though we were complete strangers to them.

Results

Of the 218 boys interviewed, 165 (76%) owned war toys and 98 (45%) wanted more of them. Of the 211 girls interviewed, 61 (29%) owned war toys and only 7 (3%) wanted more. The popularity of various war toys was as follows:

- face-to-face fighting and shooting (pistol, rifle, sword, saber, spear, bow and arrow, knife, weapon, tank) – 192 toys, 50% of the total;
- warlike male heroes (soldiers, cowboys, Indians, pirates) – 78 toys, 20% of the total;
- Star Wars, space toys – 64 toys, 17% of the total;
- other – 48 toys, 13% of the total.

Two conclusions can be drawn from these findings: (1) playing war is mostly a male thing, and (2) playing war is mostly face-to-face fighting with fantasy figures.

Table 5.1. *What children consider fun (ranked in order of popularity)*

What is fun?	No. of responses	%
Fighting (38%)		
1. Fighting	22	12
2. Aiming/shooting	17	9
3. Destroying/tearing down	14	8
4. Hiding/hunting	10	5
5. Direct aggressiveness	5	3
6. Killing	2	1
Fighting + noise (48%)		
7. Noises	19	10
Other (52%)		
8. "It looks good"	17	9
9. Winning	12	6
10. Assembling/arranging	11	6
11. Self-determination	9	5
12. Excitement	8	4
13. Feeling power	7	4
14. Technology	7	4
15. Playing with other	6	3
16. Doing away with boredom	5	3
17. Running around/rollicking	4	2
18. "One can't stop"	3	2
19. Doing forbidden things	2	1
20. No reasons	5	3
Total	185	100

Note: Items 1–7 reflect a total of 89 statements (48%) about fighting.

The discussions focused on the questions "What is fun?" and "What arguments can be found against war toys?". The first question is answered in Table 5.1. Examples of the children's responses are: "Fun is defending oneself," "Being shot at" (item 1 in the table); "Taking cover" (item 2); "The ship is sinking." "The walls of the fort are crashing down" (item 3); "We beat up each other with curtain rods. We like doing it, but I don't know why" (item

4). One can see that fun is fighting and supplying fitting sounds, onomatopoeic vocalizations such as "crash, bang, boom!" The children eagerly produced such sounds while we were speaking. One child said, "I think it's great, especially when you can make shooting sounds" (item 7).

Fun is fighting with unreal fantasy figures: cowboys, pirates, elves, Asterix and Obelix, playmobiles, and space figures. Such fighting has hardly any connection to reality and hardly shows any direct aggressiveness. The children themselves are certain about this, about the distance to reality: "It's important that one knows it is not true"; "One can live in one's fantasy"; "I prefer the weightlessness of space. In my room, I can break my nose. In space I'm weightless; nothing can happen to me there." Do war toys make children aggressive? We do not think so. They are a part of play, of "let's pretend," and most of the children know that. Fun is excitement: "action, until the last second, action!" "One doesn't know where the enemy is hiding" (item 12). Fun is deciding on your own: "I can simply do what I want to do, without parents, teachers" (item 10). Fun is the feeling of power: "One feels stronger"; "One feels like people in the movies" (item 11).

Concerning what arguments can be found against war toys, the children dealt with that topic earnestly, sometimes obviously moved. We were astonished and had difficulty with the abrupt change of atmosphere – from excited noisiness to quiet concentration. The children did not. They know the horrors or war, and they told us about them (Table 5.2): "When a nuclear bomb comes, an air-raid shelter will not help. I read in the papers that 700,000 sirens will be wailing. If there is a war, it will be a nuclear war" (item 1 in the table). "I don't like war because many people always have to die. The other people, I'm sure, would want to go on living"; "I don't like people shooting at each other, and then lying there with big wounds, still living for a little bit, and dying" (item 3).

This is reality. The children know it, and they are frightened. It seems that nobody ever speaks to them about war either. The discussions showed clearly that this reality has nothing to do with

Table 5.2. *Reasons children give against war toys*

Reasons	No. of responses	%
Statements against war (42%)		
1. War toys and war	37	25
2. Against war	20	13
3. Definite knowledge of war	6	4
Other (58%)		
4. No fun	27	18
5. Hurting	13	9
6. War toys and getting used to future violence	12	8
7. Television	10	7
8. Criticism of the meaning of war toys	9	6
9. Buying and producing war toys	4	3
10. Senselessness	3	2
11. Aspects of education	2	1
12. Preference for gender-specific games	2	1
13. Costs	2	1
14. Emotional rejection	2	1
15. War toys and direct aggressiveness	0	0

Note: Items 1–3 reflect a total of 63 statements against war toys (42%).

their play; it is only adults who get the two mixed up. If play crosses the border between fantasy and reality, it comes to an end: "I saw a war film in which bombs were dropped. And then I thought to myself, that's what I'm playing! Because of that I hate playing war now." Of course, there was also criticism of war toys, especially by the girls. It may be noted here that, in spite of such criticism, the girls still have a secret wish to participate: "My brother plays with war toys; I only watch him." "I think it's fun, but I don't play with them."

We pose the question: Do war toys make children aggressive? Not one child said so (item 5), and aren't they the ones who should know? "War toys are not good for bringing up children, and one gets nervous," said one boy. It is noteworthy that the child used the word "nervous" rather than "aggressive."

Discussion

Are these results relevant, empirically validated, and reliable? We were hunting for subjective meanings, meanings we have forgotten in our adult world. So we had to expose ourselves to the children's world of play and then try to understand. It is research according to the interpretive paradigm in the tradition of symbolic interaction (Blumer, 1973; Wilson, 1973). Any objectivity can only be discursive (see Haft, 1984), and we tried to deal with this discursive validation with thoroughness and care. We would like to stress, however, that any generalization can only be tentative.

What can parents and teachers do?

On no account should one prohibit play with war toys. I would not prevent children from playing games with combative and violent scenes. War toys are prohibited in kindergartens in Göttingen. Yet I have often seen children use bananas or switches from railroad tracks as guns. And who has not seen an index finger become a gun barrel or a hand turn into a pistol? At first, children may build a house or car with Legos, but by adding only a few pieces the structure suddenly becomes a missile with a bomb that is then dropped. Even a pistol can be quickly built – usually when the teacher is not watching. Although children know this is not allowed, that does not prevent them from doing it. On the contrary, they learn to be very clever in reinterpreting the use of the object. If an adult glances reproachfully at it, the pistol becomes a camera or a fishing rod, which, of course, has a similar appearance. The children show incredible slyness here, as well as a bit of creativity. Do we really want to encourage this slyness and this sort of creativity?

As we have shown, playing with war toys is a real game. Thus, there is apparently no reason to prohibit these toys. Adults should know that children interpret every kind of restriction and even simple intervention as violence: According to Huizinga (1956),

"Play is a free and self-determined act." Nevertheless, we are not suggesting that such play be ignored. Adults should take children's play seriously. They should speak to them about it, observe it, and try to understand it. They should accept the fascination of the game and not be envious. They should realize that teaching and information will hardly alter this fascination.

In spite of these arguments stressing freedom and self-determination in play, we hold that adults should know children's play. They must pay attention to the following points:

- Distance to reality must be maintained.
- Direct aggressiveness and brutal fantasies must not dominate the play.
- Children must not develop imaginary fears and traumas.
- War games should not become exclusive ("Playing with little soldiers makes me obsessed about it," said one girl).

Most important, adults should speak with their children about war and about everything connected to it that frightens and horrifies them. Even though this may sometimes be difficult, it is of the utmost importance. Of even greater importance is that adults openly demonstrate their desire for peace and for a nonviolent society even in cases of emergency. Positive adult models are what children need. So, adults ought to solve their own problems and worry about war and violence and their own adult world.

We had learned a lot about children's play, but it is, to be sure, a complex phenomenon; it is a strange and unknown world. Up to this point, we had only a superficial glance at it. So our second project began to evolve. We decided to observe children's free play. We tried to do this in various places but found that we needed play that occurred regularly in a closed room, which is possible in kindergartens. Anke Jaggls, Sigrun Hafa, and I were once again the members of the team.

Aggressive games of children

From January through October 1985 we conducted our study in 10 kindergartens in Göttingen. We considered the varied social and geographic districts within Göttingen, different sources of funding, and diverse educational concepts. We observed and evaluated 38 different sessions for a total of almost 42 hours. This process involved 224 boys and 215 girls (4–6 years old). Two of us (not always the same two) made verbatim written records of each play session; in most instances, we were able to complete our records. We observed the children during free play in a closed room.

The situation in the kindergartens

We were pleasantly received, but almost every kindergarten teacher and administrator began by emphasizing, "In our kindergarten, war toys are not allowed." And some added, "Children play quite peacefully in our institution." If the teachers became aware that we had observed aggressive play scenes during a session, they often seemed to be embarrassed. One teacher apologized: "I don't know at all why the kids are so aggressive today. They are normally never like this." Like war toys, aggressiveness is a delicate subject. In educational theory it is looked on as a bad thing; parents and school administrators expect there to be as little aggressiveness as possible within a group. Distinguishing among different kinds of aggressiveness is difficult, however. Often educators are very uncertain about the right way to handle aggressive situations. Nobody can blame them; it is extremely difficult. As a former teacher with classes of up to 40 children, I can speak from personal experience. Kindergarten teachers are often skeptical about educational literature and research. They feel that educational theory has often blamed the situation on them but has seldom offered plausible solutions. Our goal is to find and present such solutions.

The degree of reservation and the amount of rejection we experienced on the part of kindergarten administrators in Göttingen were shattering: "Not in our institution at all," one said to me. However, because of the courage and dedication of one truly outstanding teacher, we were able to visit her kindergarten and thus include one institution of its type in our study. Unfortunately, she was criticized by her colleagues afterward. The children usually got used to our presence readily. That we watched and took notes did not seem to bother them, and when it did, they told us so. Our respect for children's play made it possible to accept such rejection.

How did we feel and what did we experience during our observations? It was never boring. We submerged ourselves in the strange and unknown world of children's play. We were fascinated, thrilled, and touched. Time and again we became concerned: Did we have a right to intrude into this world, which belongs solely to the children and which is often – and for good reason – hidden from adult eyes? Weren't we taking advantage of the intensity of play and of the preoccupation of the players? What did we see?

Play scenes

Whipping
A respected and popular boy in the group is sitting bound to a chair and is being whipped – about 30 times with relatively hard blows – by two other boys with a leather strap. The roles are assigned: He cries out accordingly, "Ah!" "Oh!" Two girls give the bound boy some blocks as bananas to eat. The two boys wielding the whip join in and give the bound boy something imaginary to drink. The game thus experiences a resolution through which new excitement may be generated: The whipping proceeds. Obviously, all of the playmates are satisfied; the game is, for all intents and purposes, okay. When the teacher intervenes, the children become directly aggressive; chairs are thrown around, and everybody is in a bad mood.

If father and mother were dead

Two 5-year-old girls pretend that their parents have died. They formulate this play theme using the subjunctive: "If father and mother were dead, we would be alone in the woods." The abandonment is strongly emphasized. To be able to bear it, the two girls create intimacy: They make themselves extremely comfortable in a room (alone in the woods!) with flower pots, vases, and a tablecloth. They then lock everything up so that no one may come in. Even the toy rabbit helps keep watch because both of the girls are afraid of robbers. This culminates in the statement "And if they come, we'll cut their noses off!"

Making tea

A group of boys pretend to make tea, a peaceful play theme in which roles are not assigned according to gender. However, two of the boys do not accept the play idea, which originated with an unpopular boy in this group. The game degenerates into intense quarreling. Someone is constantly discriminated against in that he, for example, does not receive any tea and therefore runs screaming to the teacher. Nothing works, and the children frequently remove themselves from the game and insult one another.

Methods

Due to the spontaneity and variety of play, a standardized observational and interpretive procedure that follows strict statistical rules will hardly prove adequate. In accordance with our inquiry, it was necessary to "sample the broadest possible spectrum of the reality under investigation in the research process and concomitantly preserve the constitutional context provided by the meaningfulness in this reality" (Heinze, 1987). It was necessary to venture into the phenomenon of play with all of our senses. I shall briefly describe the procedure. (For a fuller treatment, see Wegener-Spöhring, 1989a.) The events of the game are preserved verbatim in written form as far as possible. "We sociologists have committed a great injustice, in that we have not recorded play as carefully as we have music," says Sutton-Smith (1983). We wanted to rectify this injustice.

The verbatim records (protocols) are conceived of as texts in the subsequent interpretive process, as documents to be interpreted. This documentary interpretation does not state anything about the psyche of the people at play. Game and communication patterns and rules are worked out or, to put it more correctly, construed. They are models according to which a game objectively progresses. Furthermore, the latent meaning of a game or play scene is construed. The point is to uncover the subliminal, not just the explicit, patterns and rules by which the actors (the players) play (Köckeis-Stangl, 1984). The players are usually not aware of these things. I illustrate the qualitative interpretive process with a particularly instructive example, a game called *Dracula's Grave*.

Results: balanced aggression

Dracula's Grave: interpretation of a play scene

Before the game begins, there is a phase with an unclear play theme and alternating playmates. In this situation, the attempts of several children to make social contact are ignored or rejected, aggressive acts are committed (bricks are thrown around; a boy pushes a girl out of a box), and conflicts are resolved through crying and tattling on the others. Then a boy and a girl, who have just treated one another aggressively, form a play group and now integrate their play wishes – Dracula's grave and family. They add a scatological theme to this game that they play together (toilet, peeing, stinking, farting sounds), a strong lion, and a witch. The main theme, however, is that Dracula's grave is erected with bricks and then torn down again – "smashed up," as the children say. They regulate these tension curves (activation circles) in complete agreement, conflicts are present only within the game (e.g., whether or not the father is on the toilet), and the interaction is friendly, cooperative, and imaginative. Both children are completely absorbed in the play. Aside from their building activity, they speak and act in various roles. The frightening and aggressive themes of the Dracula game are continually toned down, made tolerable, and "balanced" by associating them with the family game. At the game's climax the cannibalism theme surfaces. After three different versions it culminates in the following scene:

> *Girl:* "Children, do you know what? We're going to go to a mean kid and eat him."
>
> *Boy:* "Yeah, sure."
>
> *Girl:* "I'll get a kid. See you later. Here I am again. Dracula [gets] a piece, you a piece – umm, umm."

Immediately after this brutal and shocking scene, the girl directs their play by connecting it to the family game in a familiar and positive direction: "Dracula, do you want to marry me? Dracula, do all of us want to live here together?" The boy reinforces this theme and then distances himself from the game by abandoning the role: "They get married then" (he says "they," not "we"). The play balance is reestablished; the immense tension of the preceding scene is satisfactorily resolved. Afterward the boy and girl jointly allow the game to end and even clear away the building blocks.

This excellent dramaturgy is realized on the level of latent meaning and reveals itself, little by little, to the researcher conducting the interpretation. It should be noted that this play transcript, like all others, is always rather confused at first, so that the interpretive process begins in a state of helplessness.

I now describe the constitution of the play theme in detail and thereby explain our methodological procedure.

The verbatim record:
> *Boy:* 1. "I like animals.
> 2. Where Dracula lives.
> 3. He lives in a grave.
> 4. Dracula is strong.

5. My dad is stronger than Dracula; your father too.
6. He (the girl's father/Dracula?) is dead already.
7. I'll build Dracula's grave."

Interpretation:
Boy: 1. Takes up an earlier play idea from the girl and strengthens it (animals).
2. Introduces a new, fantastic, and frightening play topic → introduction of the play theme.
3. Expresses knowledge of Dracula.
4. Emphasis of his strength, probably frightening.
5. Weakening of the strength by something familiar to himself and the girl (family) [*Balance*].
6. Not interpreted.
7. Play idea → introduces the final play theme.

One sees how much social competence the boy uses and how much effort he expends to win over the girl for his game. Even afterward she first just looks on while he builds something; therefore, the following sequences contain additional balancing and integration achievements by the boy until the girl is ready to integrate herself into the game.

I now present another sequence occurring at the climax of their play.

The verbatim record:
Girl: 1. "Old train."
Boy: 2. "Ancient, like great-grandmother."
Girl: 3. "Where is Dracula?
4. You take care of the children when the lion comes."
Boy: 5. (With a deep voice) "Yeah, sure."
Girl: 6. "I also brought some cars."
7. The boy talks about something that stinks and about shit (not transcribed verbatim).

Boy: 8. "Where's the father?"
Girl: 9. "He's taking a shit."
Boy: 10. "On the pot.
         11. Help, the grave of Dracula!
         12. Come on, let's keep playing."
Girl: 13. "Come on, smash everything up!"
         14. Both of them knock everything down.

Interpretation:
Girl: 1. A new play idea.
Boy: 2. Seizes on this and develops it.
Girl: 3. Continues the boy's play idea.
           4. New play idea: symbol of strength refers to her family game. Makes a role – specific request of the boy.
Boy: 5. Accepts this and assumes the role.
Girl: 6. New play idea that does not coincide with the play theme (car).
Boy: 7. Ignores this; refers to his own play idea (fecal game).
           8. Refers to the play of the girl (family) [*Balance*].
Girl: 9. She accepts this; drops her car play idea.
Boy: 10. Continues the fecal game in slightly weakened form.
          11. Resumes the main theme, with emphasis ("help").
          12. Urges that they continue playing (building).
Girl: 13. Follows up on this request in terms of the previous play ("smashing up...").
Girl/Boy: 14. Terminate the activation circle [*AC*].

This is a dramatic play scene containing an extremely rapid sequence of play elements with a climax and an end. And immediately afterward, it continues: "Come on, let's build it even prettier!" The fact that the girl does not have play capabilities equal to those of the boy (this will be obvious in other sequences of their play as well) is irrelevant. The boy overlooks her inadequate play suggestion, and both participants are at once carried away by the dynamics of their play.

I now summarize the interpretative results of the game Dracula's grave and add further results obtained on the topic of aggression. In particular, I refer to the play scenes presented initially.

Propositions regarding balanced aggression

Children balance that which is aggressive, frightening, and indecent in good play so that all participants can tolerate it and nobody has to stop playing. In the game of whipping, the person who is tied up receives something to eat and drink at a critical point. The girls alone in the woods live as securely as they can in their frightening situation. This balancing is a complex achievement, requiring a great deal of social competence from the participants.

In good play, aggressive acts remain at the "let's pretend" level and do not interfere with the friendly interaction of participants at play. This is just barely true of the game of whipping; we have often observed this kind of "tightrope walking." If an adult interferes, however, he or she probably destroys the finely spun pattern of playful balance. This also was apparent in the game of whipping. Disturbances of the balance, however, necessarily lead to disturbances of play and stagnation, and often also to play-external aggression and conflicts.

In good play, conflicts also remain play-immanent. In the game of being alone in the woods, there are many examples of this:

Girl₂: "The door has to be there; otherwise, the rabbit will run away."
Girl₁: "I have a better idea."
Girl₂: "No."
Girl₁: "The rabbit will always stay with us."

Girl₂: "Yes."

Girl₁: "Or it can sometimes run away; it will always come back."

Girl₂: "Yes."

(Girl₁ and Girl₂ come to the table and get a basket there and a department store catalog.)

Girl₁: "I'll see what nice things we have there."

Girl₂: "What we can cut out."

Girl₁: "We're not going to cut anything out."

Girl₂: "Look, look. Do we want to buy this kind of rabbit?"

Girl₁: "An all-white one would be better."

Girl₂: "Yeah, they have that too."

Differences of opinion and conflicts can remain play-immanent because they become unimportant through adequate integration of the play wishes. A counterexample is the game of making tea, presented earlier.

Boy₁, Boy₂, and Boy₃ demonstrate, by looking around the room at the beginning of play, that they no longer desire to make tea. The small boy, Boy_sm, meanwhile sets the table. Then he leaves. Boy₁ and Boy₂ clear the table and, while doing this, say: "Let's get this stuff off the table. There's a spider, there's an ant." Boy_sm returns but doesn't say anything. The four boys sit around the cleared table. Boy₁ says: "I am Ali from the *Muppet Show*."

The teacher had suggested that they continue making tea. Boy₁ and Boy₂ throw the dishes while they set the table. Boy₃ starts to cry and says to the teacher: "Alex [Boy₂] is always so mean to me." The teacher does not respond and leaves. Boy₁ has a milk jug and says: "The drinks are on me, boys."

Boy₁: "Everyone plays when I'm here."

Boy₂: "I'll get the police."

Boy₃: (Whining) "Leave me alone. I don't want to have anything to do with you. You're stupid assholes."

Boy₂: "You're getting into a jeep with a bomb in it."
Boy₃: "Leave me alone."

When the water for the tea, despite all the hindrances, finally begins to boil, the tea cannot be made because the tea bag is gone. Instead, the following discussion takes place:

Boy₂: "I'm a hitta, pishsh."
Boy₃: "Can I be a hitta too?"
Boy₂: "No."

Boy₃ pinches Boy₂; Boy₂ begins to cry. Boy₁ takes revenge on Boy₃ on behalf of Boy₂; a small fight takes place.

Boy₃: "Two to one is not fair."
Boy₁: "I know."
Boy₃: "I'm going to tell on you."

All four boys sit down again at the table. Boy₃ says to Boy₂: "But see what happens if you poke me in the stomach with your pocket knife." Although they have almost finished making tea, the tea bag has fallen into the teapot and has to be extricated from the hot water. The boys, one after another, burn their fingers. During the distribution of the tea, the small boy doesn't get any; the teacher intervenes.

 This is play, which none of the participants wants, apart from the small boy. Play in which the play wishes are not integrated and aggression, which is not tied to the play but is play-external, lead to injuries and hurt feelings.

 Aggressive play does not reproduce reality; no play does this. A transformation into a play reality always occurs, either by use of the subjunctive ("If Dad and Mom were dead, we would be alone in the woods"), by demonstrating the assumption of roles (the disguised deep voice in the Dracula game), or by laughing, as did the girl who aimed the trunk of the stuffed elephant at me. The message is: This is play!

*Children deal with aggressive themes in their play in various ways. These themes surface in play, disappear again without large breaks, and are possibly renewed and reintroduced in another form: Dracula and family, robbers and rabbit, whipping and taking care of the person whipped. And the trunk of the elephant, just mentioned, is immediately used for drinking again after it has been used for shooting.

*Aggressive play is simply fun. It is dynamic, exciting, and usually strongly physical. It is action accompanied by laughter, cries, and onomatopoeic vocalization.

It is amazing to observe how imaginative and expressive the children are in the production of these onomatopoeic noises. The noises can hardly be spelled out with letters. Prototypes of this simple, aggressive play are cars flipping over, pillow fights, cutting up mattresses, and a playful power struggle.

*Because it is so dynamic and exciting in a simple way, aggressive play usually appears as a theme that enables a child to participate easily. Each participant knows immediately what is going on: pursuit/flight; chasing/becoming a prisoner; hiding/being found again; shooting/being hit; aiming–hitting/destroying. These are well-known basic patterns that function immediately. An explanation is not required. For this reason, aggressive play themes are also advantageous as connecting links in play situations where there is disagreement about the organization and rules of play:

Four boys are playing with building blocks and cars; a ramp has already been built for the cars. One boy does not want to allow any changes to be made on the ramp; a fight is in the making. Another boy pushes his car into a building block: "Crash, crash..." That is funny; all of them laugh; the fight doesn't occur; the boys continue playing.

I will not discuss whether or not playful aggression serves to make children feel strong and powerful, and helps them to master their fears and nightmares, as I have previously maintained. I have often seen how the doll was kicked, the car thrown against the wall, the rabbit pounded, the teddy bear hung up by its ear. Since the child had the teddy bear cry out "Ouch, yow" during this act, little doubt remains with respect to the aggressive intent directed at the toy. There are probably diverse reasons for this aggression; however, we don't know what they are. Nevertheless, it can perhaps be maintained that children at play anticipatively test the interaction with themes and subjects that they do not usually encounter in reality, yet that preoccupy and disturb them: death, injury, fighting and war, violence, fear, being left alone: "If Dad and Mom were dead..."

Conclusion: good or bad play

The question concerning good or bad play does not involve the theme of the play; the quality of play is decided at the level of interaction.

- Good play is characterized by a sensible dramaturgy, a complicated web of relations, and a complex thematic structure.
- The ways in which children regulate or organize their playful interactions are of decisive importance.
- Maintaining the balance of play and creation of the "let's pretend" level of play in particular are of decisive importance.
- In addition, it is necessary for the play participants to be proficient in various techniques of play (e.g., the ability to assume and abandon roles; the ability to identify and reinterpret play objects). They must also be able to introduce new phases into their play and create good play arrangements.

Good play is that which all enjoy. Children naturally like to play good games; they therefore are eager to learn how.

We also observed children who did not possess these capabilities or whose proficiency was limited – children who do not adequately integrate their desire for play, who do not make play suggestions that are appropriate with respect to the situation and the roles involved, who cannot adequately deal with or accept the suggestions made by other children for play, and who destroy play by mixing play with reality. These children need our protection and help, help requiring competence derived from educational science and the educational theory of play. I will never forget the girl who, during the entire phase of free play, did not produce one idea for play, did not participate anywhere, and hardly spoke with any other child. Finally she sat down on a game board, bent and curled up like a banana and, beaming, said, because of this idea, "Look, Nicole" to the girl standing next to her. Nicole, who was a friendly and socially competent child, responded, however: "I don't want to look at all."

Although we conducted our observations for nearly 42 hours, questions remain to be answered. Researchers in educational science and educational theory of play should make every effort to unlock the wonderful world of play for children, too, who are like the girl we just described. And this world *is* wonderful even if it appears chaotic and wild.

One last example:

Boy₁: (Cries out) "Jackass, wienie, brutal snail, plucked chicken."
(Boy₂ and Boy₃ return.) "I kept a good lookout, nobody came."

Boy₃: (Cries out) "War!"
(Then he runs away. Boy₂ runs after him. Both of them then return.)

Boy₂: "I strapped my gun to my back."

Boy₃: "Do you see the dead man down there?"

Boy₂: "Yeah. A bandit."

Boy₃: "We can take his gun."

Boy₂: "You mean his knife."

Boy₃: "Yeah, and his pistols and helmet and belt and ar-
          mor."
Boy₂: "Bandits don't have any armor."
          (Boy₂ and Boy₃ go down and carry out their play
          idea.)
Boy₃: "Into the ammunition room."

"Play is the sphere in which the unspoken finds expression . . .
and unrecognized desires are satisfied" (Sutton-Smith, 1983). As
adults and educators, we have always had difficulty with this idea.

6

Sex differences in toy play and use of video games

JEFFREY H. GOLDSTEIN

Should parents worry about their 6-year-old son who plays with dolls or their daughter who prefers football to Barbie? Is it natural for boys to play more aggressively than girls or to sequester themselves in their rooms playing video games? This chapter is about differences and similarities in the play of boys and girls. We begin by examining different views of children's play and how these are influenced by our attitudes and personal experiences.

Looking at children's play

Boys and girls play differently, and men and women differ in their views of that play. This can be seen clearly by examining aggressive play.

Boys' play, far more often than the play of girls, is viewed as a form of, or bordering on, real violence. Recent books by Nancy Carlsson-Paige and Diane Levin (1987, 1990), Myriam Miedzian (1991), and Pamela Tuchscherer (1988) lament the aggressiveness that they believe is ingrained in boys' toys, video games, and play.

Concern about aggressive play is based on the assumptions that such play is learned, that it can be inhibited or suppressed, and that it contributes to later real aggression. Some of these observers do not distinguish between aggressive *play* and aggressive *behav-*

ior, seeing them as one and the same.[1] There is no doubt that
aggressive play is unseemly; during it, children run around and
make noise. There is enough anarchy in such play to entice some
observers to label it *aggression*.

Observers of children's play often comment on how rarely fighting actually takes place among boys engaged in play fighting (Fry,
1990; Pellegrini, 1988; Smith, this volume; Sutton-Smith, Gerstmyer & Meckley, 1988; Wegener-Spöhring, 1989a, and this volume). To most children, fighting and play fighting are two different
things. In fact, the most aggressive children appear *least* likely to
engage in play fighting (Willner, 1991), perhaps because highly
aggressive children violate the shared, if unstated, rules of aggressive play, particularly the idea that one is not supposed to injure
playmates.

At least three characteristics influence the degree to which children's play and toys are viewed as aggressive: the *age* and *sex* of
observers and their *prior experiences* with toys and rough play.
There are probably other elements that influence these judgments
– for example, the observer's own level of aggression and the
setting (home, playground, classroom) in which the children play
– but these have not been studied systematically.

Children and adults view play differently

Anthropologists know that observing a culture from the outside
is not the same as experiencing it from the inside. These two
perspectives result in different pictures of the culture, which are
not always compatible with one another. There are also two views
of children's play: those of the adult observer and of the child
participant (Sneed & Runco, 1992).

Adults and children differ in their views of aggressive play.
Children distinguish between aggressive play and real violence.

---

[1] *Aggressive behavior* or *aggression* is the attempt to injure another person. *Aggressive play*, *play fighting*, *rough-and-tumble play*, and *war play* involve the imaginative or pre-tended use of aggression; there is no attempt to injure.

Studies of children in England (Jukes, 1991; Smith & Boulton, 1990), Germany (Wegener-Spöhring, 1989a), Mexico (Fry, 1990), and the United States (Pellegrini, 1988; Sutton-Smith et al., 1988) found in each case that children reliably distinguish play fighting from real fighting.

Parents and teachers, who view children's play from a distance, seem less often to make the distinction between play fighting and actual fighting. A study in Great Britain and Italy found that parents do not consistently see aggressive play and aggression differently (Costabile, Genta, Zucchini, Smith & Harker 1992). Of course, there are inevitable similarities between play fighting and real fighting, such as chasing, fleeing, and wrestling, that occur during both. Boys generally agree that play fighting can become real aggression, particularly when accidental injury occurs. This happens only occasionally, according to studies by Fry (1990), Humphreys and Smith (1987), Pellegrini (1988), and Sutton-Smith et al. (1988). Play fighting may turn into aggression when adults break the "play frame" of the children, for example, by chastising them for fighting when they are merely playing (Wegener-Spöhring, 1989a).

Women "see" more aggression than do men

Among adults, the perception of aggression in children's play depends in part on whether the observer is a man or a woman. Kathleen Connor (1989) videotaped 4- and 5-year-olds playing with toy trucks, dolls, and crayons (neutral toys) or with GI Joe, Rambo with guns, and grenades (war toys). Fourteen of these play episodes were shown to male and female university students, who classified each as play or aggression. Males and females viewed 10 of the 14 episodes differently. For example, in one incident, two boys and a girl are playing with toy guns. They decide that shooting a "dead" person with his own weapon restores him to life. In the incident, a "dead" boy is shot and revived in this way.

Seventy-five percent of the males viewed this as playful compared to only 38% of the females. "Aggression is in the eye of the beholder," writes Connor (1989); females in comparison to males are more likely to label an episode as aggression.

Connor asked her adult subjects whether they had played with war toys as children. Women who had played with such toys as children, usually because they had brothers who engaged them in war play, were less apt to label an episode of children's rough play as aggression. This result highlights the importance of personal experience in interpreting children's play.

The role of prior experience

The classic study of the influence of attitudes on perception of a game was conducted by Hastorf and Cantril (1954) at an American college football game. In 1951, Dartmouth College lost an important football game to Princeton University. It was a particularly rough game, in which Princeton's All-American quarterback received a broken nose and a Dartmouth player suffered a broken leg. A week after the game, students at each school were shown a film of the game and told to note any rule violations they observed. When Dartmouth students viewed the film, they noted an average of 4.3 violations by the Dartmouth team. When Princeton students viewed the same film, they noted 9.8 infractions by the Dartmouth team. Hastorf and Cantril concluded that "there is no such thing as a 'game' existing 'out there' in its own right which people merely observe."

What Hastorf and Cantril wrote of American football is apt to be even more true of unfamiliar or less organized games, such as those children play on the playground. Unless one knows the rules of a football game – both the written rules and the informal, implicit ones – it would seem like meaningless chaos. Unless an observer understands the implicit rules of children's war play, for example, it too is apt to appear chaotic and undisciplined.

Play styles of boys and girls

Boys and girls tend to play differently and prefer different play-things (Goldstein, 1992; Moller, Hymel & Rubin, 1992). In a study of the games of American boys and girls, Lever (1978) concluded that the games played by boys were more complex, with a larger number of roles, more participants, and more explicit goals, and more often involved the formation of teams. Moller et al. (1992) also found more group play among 7- to 9-year-old boys than among girls, as well as more functional and exploratory play. Lever writes that these differences in play may contribute to sex differences in adulthood in such areas as competition, leadership, and styles of human relationships.

Rough-and-tumble play

Rough-and-tumble play, such as play wrestling, is primarily the prerogative of boys (DiPietro, 1981; Fry, 1990; Pellegrini, 1988). As with war play, some psychologists argue that rough-and-tumble play leads to subsequent real aggression (Carlsson-Paige & Levin, 1987, 1990; Miedzian, 1991). Others state that such play contributes to social and emotional development (Bettelheim, 1987; Sutton-Smith & Kelly-Byrne, 1984; Sutton-Smith et al., 1988). According to Pellegrini (1988), this confusion results partly from "definitional problems." Some researchers define rough-and-tumble play to include both fighting and mock fighting. Some count both verbal and physical attacks as aggression.

   While viewing German school children at play, Gisela Wegener-Spöhring (1989a) counted 62 aggressive incidents by girls and 335 by an equal number of boys. "Are boys therefore five times as bad as girls? Certainly not." Boys are allowed and expected to display more aggressive behavior than girls. Girls are still supposed to be obedient and passive, and ashamed of being aggressive and quarrelsome, she notes. Bjorkqvist, Lagerspetz and Kaukiainen (1991) found that girls are aggressive in ways that do not include the masculine forms of overt violence. For example, social ostracism and gossip are used often by girls to injure other girls (Bjorkqvist & Niemela, 1992).

Toy preference

Among children in the United States, preference for sex-typed toys first appears at about 2 years of age, although it has been observed in children as young as 18 months (Caldera, Huston & O'Brien, 1989; Fein, Johnson, Kosson, Stork & Wasserman 1985; Weintraub et al., 1984). Sex-stereotyped play tends to increase with age, perhaps because of the influence of parents and peers (Moller et al., 1992; Serbin, Conner, Burchardt & Citron, 1979).

Girls tend to choose dolls and household objects, and boys soldiers and trucks. Girls also choose masculine toys, though not as consistently as do boys (Almqvist, 1989a; Eisenberg, Wolchik, Hernandez & Pasternack, 1985). Adventure themes, fantasy characters, superheroes, spacemen, and television-inspired roles comprise the favored fantasy games of boys; girls show a preference for family roles (pretending to be mother, father, baby), "house" games, and dress-up clothes. These sex differences were noted in research as early as 1933 by Parten.

These observations are not limited to the United States; similar patterns of sex-typed play and toy preferences have been reported for European and Asian children (Suito & Reifel, 1992; Wegener-Spöhring, 1989a; Zammuner, 1987; see also Roopnarine, Ahmeduzzaman, Hossain & Reigraf, 1992). Zammuner (1987) found that the sex-role beliefs of European children resemble those of their parents.

There are both immediate and delayed effects of sex-typed toy play. During and immediately following play with such toys, children are more accepted by their peers, who are more likely to approach them (Berndt & Heller, 1986; Moller et al., 1992). Furthermore, teachers tend to leave children alone if they are playing with sex-typed toys (Fagot, 1984). According to Parker (1984), the long-term effect of sex-typed play is to prepare children for their adult roles as men and women.

Boys and war toys

It is primarily boys who engage in rough-and-tumble play, war games, and fantasy aggression.[2] For instance, in interviews with 10-year-old German children, Wegener-Spöhring (1989a) found that 76% of the boys owned toy guns compared with 29% of the girls.

Jacqueline Jukes (1991) studied the conditions under which war toys are preferred to other types of playthings. For boys, but not for girls, chronic level of aggression was significantly correlated with a preference for aggressive toys: Aggressive boys preferred aggressive toys.

If children are first "primed" with aggressive stories, they are more likely to choose toy weapons for play (Jukes & Goldstein, 1993; Lovaas, 1961). The reasoning underlying this research is the notion that exposure to violence in the media or in reality primes, or activates, aggressive associations. These, in turn, will heighten the preference for further exposure to violence (Berkowitz, 1984). Priming effects are known to affect the preference for violent film entertainment (Langley, O'Neal, Craig & Yost, 1992). One study reported an increase in attendance at violent films by University of Wisconsin students following the murder of a student on campus (Boyanowsky, Newtson & Walster, 1974). In an early study of toy selection, Lovaas (1961) found that exposure to a violent film increased the preference for aggressive toys among 5-year-old children. There is also anecdotal evidence to support the priming position: During the 1991 war in the Persian Gulf, sales of replica weapons skyrocketed, so to speak, though the market for these expensive models consisted largely of adults.

---

[2]The focus in this section is on why children choose to play with war toys. The *effects* of war play are considered in the chapters by Peter K. Smith and by Gisela Wegener-Spöhring in this volume.

According to Singer and Singer (1990), the play styles of American boys and girls are converging. They write that girls are

> moving closer to boys in their identification with heroic figures, adventurous achievement, and pretend aggression than previous data claimed. This appears to reflect changes in television action programs, where more female heroines now appear, as well as the increased willingness of parents to tolerate adventure themes in girls play. . . . We do not see a comparable trend among boys – that is, a move toward playing female games and using traditionally female toys. (p. 80)

Although the play styles and toy preferences of boys and girls may be merging, differences still exist. Children develop stereotypes of appropriate play for boys and girls early in life. Children as young as age 5 have views on "appropriate" play for boys and girls (Carvalho, Smith, Hunter & Costabile, 1990).

Boys and girls differ not only in their preference for rough play and war toys, but also in their attachment to and interest in video and computer games.

Video and computer games

Sex differences in video game play

Despite repeated efforts to increase the appeal of video games to girls, the crowds around the games in toy stores and video arcades are composed mainly of boys. Kubey and Larson (1990) report that 80% of video game play among children 9–15 years of age is by boys.

Until about 10 years of age, girls seem to have as much fascination as boys with computers. If video games are the point of entry into the world of computers, as Patricia Marks Greenfield (1984) maintains, then the fact that so many of these games involve aggressive fantasy themes may have the effect of turning girls away from computers in general (Kinder, 1991; Provenzo, 1991). When an aggressive fantasy theme was added to a video game, boys liked the game more, and girls less, than the same game without an aggressive theme (Malone, 1981).

Girls become more interested in computers connected to programmable "digital trains" (Catherall, 1989). These are computer-operated trains for which children are the "engineers," able to control over 250 accessory devices, such as switches and signals. This places demands on players to cooperate in a play atmosphere. In school settings, girls are no less interested than boys in programming the trains.

A study by Cooper, Hall and Huff (1990) found that girls experienced increased stress when using computer software that appeals to boys. Boys reported more stress than girls when working with female-oriented programs. In their study, 52 boys and girls in sixth through eighth grades (aged 11–14 years) used mathematics programs with themes that appeal either mainly to boys (shooting or propelling objects through fantasy space, graphic feedback, action, aggression) or mainly to girls (absence of aggression/shooting, verbal feedback, cooperative). These programs were used either in isolation or in a computer room with other students nearby. In the social setting, girls experienced greater stress using "masculine programs" and boys felt greater stress using "feminine programs." The authors express the view that basing educational materials on video arcade games may increase stress in girls and contribute to their avoidance of computers. It is noteworthy that the effects were obtained only when children were in the presence of their schoolmates. This suggests the important role played by potential peer disapproval.

Video games may influence players in at least two ways. First, the act of playing video games itself may affect players. For example, people may use their leisure time differently, perhaps watching less television or going to the movies less often. Playing computer and video games may increase hand–eye coordination and facility with computer programming. Second, there may be effects of specific video games or video-game genres, for example, those with violent, competitive, or sexist themes.

Social effects: isolation and sociability

Parents sometimes fear that video game play isolates their children. Gerard Bonnafont (1992), in a cohort study of 300 French school children, reports two effects on the social behavior of video game players:

1. *Parent–child communication* may be disrupted as a result of video game play. Bonnafont believes that this occurs because parents often do not understand the games, exclude themselves from the video game culture, and may be unable to compete successfully with their children.
2. *Video games increase social contact among peers.* Video games create conviviality among children, who play the games together, exchange information and game cassettes, and create clubs around video games. Paradoxically, even though video games may be played in isolation, they are the focus of social contact for many boys. In a sense, video games are the most social media. A study of American children aged 9–15 found that video games were played alone 46.5% of the time, but they were played with friends (35.6%) more than twice as often as engagement in any other media activity (Kubey & Larson, 1990).

In a Canadian study of arcade video game players, game playing did not dominate the leisure patterns of youth (Ng, 1990). Nor did home video games in a U.S. study by Kubey and Larson (1990). Video game play accounted for only 3.3% of all media time, whereas traditional television viewing accounted for three-fourths of media use.

As with anything, excessive use of video games may have adverse consequences. First, there will be physical and visual fatigue and headaches from excessive play (Bonnafont, 1992). Second, some children may become obsessed with video games. In Bonnafont's research, 20–25% of video game players may be classified as "passionate" players. It would be troubling if video games were the child's sole source of leisure-time activity, or if they were used to avoid contact with family members or schoolmates.

Pediatrician Barton D. Schmitt (1992) has suggestions for parents whose children spend a disproportionate amount of time playing computer/video games: (1) Establish rules for game play – for example, only after homework or chores are completed; (2) limit playing time; (3) take advantage of the educational games and software available; (4) encourage a variety of leisure activities – music, reading, hobbies, sports, outdoor activities.

School performance

Bonnafont (no date) examined the use of video games by French school children who received good or poor grades. The 7- to 12-year-olds with poor grades did not play video games more often than those with good grades: Both groups tended to play video games 8 to 15 hours per week.

Creasey and Myers (1986) studied the effects of acquiring a home video game system. They examined relationships among the novelty of the video system, time spent playing video games, involvement in other leisure activities, peer interactions, homework time, and grades. Using questionnaires completed by sixty-four 9- to 16-year-olds, they found that within a few weeks to a few months of acquisition, children moved from intense interest in playing video games back to their typical pattern of activities, with no measurable change in academic functioning.

There was a relationship in one study between time spent in video *arcades* and lowered academic performance in mathematics (Lin & Lepper, 1987). But there was no such relationship for video games played *at home*. Parental attitude toward school perfor-

mance is known to be a major factor in academic success. Therefore, the lack of parental monitoring that is typical of arcade play
must be considered (Funk, 1992).

Cognitive effects

An understanding of video game performance may increase our
knowledge of *human performance:*

> Students of human perception and human performance may
> benefit from a serious consideration of video games in terms of
> information processing and motor skills. The various skills that
> underlie successful performance in games that emphasize de-
> tecting, monitoring, tracking, and intercepting moving targets
> appear to be important for successful performance in other tasks
> as well. For example, a series of human performance studies
> show that a particular video game (Atari *Air Combat Maneu-
> vering Task*) measures essentially the same skills as a simple
> compensatory tracking task used to train naval aviators and
> measures them more reliably. (Brown, Brown & Reid, 1992).

In order to uncover the logic of a computer game, children use
inductive reasoning. They must remember responses, sequences,
and answers discovered earlier. Memory and attention are thus
required. Furthermore, children learn to think in a scientific way:
They analyze known features of the game, create a working hypothesis, and check its validity against the reality of the game. "It
might be this fact – that intelligence is expressed by an action
rather than an idea – that makes some people think that intelligence
does not play any role here" (Bonnafont, 1992). One characteristic
of intelligence is the ability to adapt to new situations, a feature
of video games.

Despite its classroom potential, the use of video games to teach
traditional school subjects may be further away than is supposed
by many of those working in the field of interactive technologies,

according to Gabriel Jacobs (1992). The history of education shows a long-standing rejection of teaching based on discovery, exploration, and individual experience.

Personality and psychopathology

"Despite initial concern, current research suggests that even frequent video game playing bears no significant relationship to the development of true psychopathology" (Funk, 1992). Kestenbaum and Weinstein (1985), for example, failed to identify expected increases in withdrawal and social isolation in frequent game players. Attempts also have been made to describe the frequent video game player's characteristic personality profile. Findings to date have been both contradictory and inconclusive (Kestenbaum & Weinstein, 1985; Lin & Lepper, 1987).

Aggression and video games

Video game research is often modeled on television violence research. But the effects of video games appear to be more similar to those of aggressive toys than to those of violent television programs. In his review of video games and aggression, Provenzo (1991) concludes that "research conducted up to this time on video games suggests that while the games probably do not contribute significantly to deviant behavior, they do – at least on a short-term basis – increase the aggressive behavior of the individuals who play them." This conclusion mirrors the effects of war toys, which also seem to give rise to short-lived increases in aggressive behavior (Goldstein, 1992).

The video game–television comparison may be inappropriate. There are important differences between playing video games and watching television. Among other things, there are differences in *content* and in the *social setting* in which these media are used. Furthermore, television viewing is a relatively passive activity, whereas video game playing is more *active,* with choices, responses, and controls in the hands of the players.

Differences in content

Television frequently presents scenes of actual or enacted violence, in contrast to video game violence, which is generally on an abstract fantasy level. Because video game violence is not as realistic as television violence, it is not as easily learned or imitated. Furthermore, the fantasy characters of video games often seek to *avoid* violence.

Video games with fighting/war themes are being increasingly replaced by strategic games of the Tetris variety, according to Bonnafont (1992).

Activity and control

Video/computer game players, in contrast to television viewers, exert *control* over what takes place on the screen. They are participants in an interactive system that allows them to regulate the pace and character of the game. This, in turn, gives them increased control over their own emotional states during play. Presumably, children will play with the degree of involvement and activity that is most pleasing to them (Zillmann, 1991). This means that the same game may be played for excitement or relaxation, depending on the player's wishes and the ways in which he or she interacts with the game.

Differences in social setting

Video games typically involve *cooperation* among players, whereas television viewing does not. Regarding *social interaction,* Greenfield (1984) notes that a two-person aggressive game, video boxing, does not increase aggression, whereas a solitary aggressive game, Space Invaders, may stimulate further aggression. "Perhaps the effects of television in stimulating aggression will also be found to stem partly from the fact that television viewing typically involves little social interaction."

Origins of sex differences in play

How does a toy become sex-typed? Recent studies suggest that both biological and social processes play a role in toy preference and play style (Goldstein, 1992).

Biological foundations of sex differences in play and toy preference

Erik Erikson (1977) asserted that differences in children's play are an outgrowth of the biological, more precisely morphological, differences between the sexes. He observed that young boys build vertical constructions that involve active themes, whereas girls construct enclosures with static themes. Girls' creations were said to mirror the passive, enclosed nature of female genitalia, whereas boys' constructions reflect the intrusive, erect nature of the penis. Needless to say, such a pointed argument is controversial (Rubin, Fein & Vandenberg, 1983).

Meyer-Bahlburg, Feldman, Cohen and Ehrhardt (1988) have documented a relationship between prenatal exposure to a synthetic female hormone, progestogen, and a reduction in rough-and-tumble play in both sexes. This suggests that some of the difference between the play of boys and girls is due to biological factors.

Toy preference, too, may be influenced by biology. For example, a child with a high need for movement and activity may like to play with traditionally masculine toys because they permit highly active play. Activity level tends to be higher in boys, who select toys that permit more active types of play (Eaton & Enns, 1986; Maccoby & Jacklin, 1974).

More specific toy preferences have also been related to prenatal exposure to hormones. Both boys and girls exposed prenatally and in the early postnatal months to high levels of the male hormone androgen showed a greater preference for traditionally boys' toys at ages 3 to 8 years (Berenbaum & Hines, 1992).

Social foundations

Early exposure to particular hormones plays a role in children's play styles and toy preferences. So, too, does early exposure to models, to the behavior of those – parents and peers – around the child.

Whether a toy is perceived as appropriate for a boy or a girl is determined partly by the child's same-sex peers. In a study by Shell and Eisenberg (1990), 4- and 5-year olds viewed a toy as a boys' toy if they had previously observed mainly boys playing with the toy and as a girls' toy if girls had been seen playing with it. Children tend to avoid the toy preferences of peers of the other sex (Ruble, Balaban & Cooper, 1981).

When children choose toys considered appropriate for their sex, playmates of the same sex approach them (Eisenberg, Tryon & Cameron, 1984; Moller et al., 1992). Indeed, among the reasons for making these toy choices may be the desire for peer approval, the wish to avoid negative reactions from peers, and the desire to engage in further interactions with peers of the same sex (Shell & Eisenberg, 1990).

Parents are also sex-role models for their children. According to Catherine Garvey (1991), sex-typed toy preferences are due to "parents' influence as models and to their approval or support of children's interest in sex-stereotyped objects."

Many studies report that parents are likely to purchase sex-typed toys for their children, particularly if the parents themselves hold traditional sex-role attitudes (Eckerman & Stein, 1990; O'Brien & Huston, 1985; Rheingold & Cook, 1975; Zammuner, 1987). Not surprisingly, children who choose traditional sex-typed toys are more likely to have parents who hold traditional attitudes about sex roles (Repetti, 1984).

Women who expressed a belief in sex differences were more

likely to choose a toy hammer when asked to interact with an infant labeled as a boy, whereas women who expressed little belief in sex differences were not affected in their choice of toy by knowledge of the infant's sex (Bell & Carver, 1980).

Perhaps the most striking example of parental influence is provided in a study of the rooms of 96 children aged from under 1 to 6 years, from middle-class American families (Rheingold & Cook 1975). There was no great difference between the boys' and girls' rooms with respect to the presence of books, furniture, musical objects, and stuffed animals. Boys' rooms contained far more toy animals in barns or zoos, as well as objects relating to space, energy, or time (magnets, puzzles, space ships). Girls' rooms contained more dolls. Even though boys' rooms contained some dolls (e.g., GI Joe, cowboys), virtually none represented females or babies. The most extreme difference was in the number of vehicles owned by the boys (375) compared to the girls (17). No girl had a wagon, bus, motorcycle, boat, or trailer. The typical boy of 2 had at least 3 vehicles and by the age of 3 had an average of 11. Only boys had live animals, depots, replicas of heavy equipment, and military toys; only girls had doll houses, stoves, tea sets, and cradles for dolls.

One of the researchers had previously observed in her laboratory that girls of 18 months spent as much time playing with trucks as boys did. She concludes that parents were not responding to the spontaneous interests of their children but were themselves primarily responsible for the extremely different inventories of objects found in the boys' and girls' rooms.

Adults pass their own sex-role attitudes on to children, along with the toys they give to them. As these attitudes change among parents, they are reflected in their toy purchases for children. As observed by Singer and Singer (1990), girls are increasingly likely to play with traditionally boys' toys, and parents are increasingly willing to purchase such toys for them. This suggests that the play of girls is becoming broader, incorporating traditionally masculine forms of play into their repertoire without abandoning traditionally feminine play.

Not only do adults buy different toys for their sons and daughters, but they also play differently with them. American fathers spend an average of 50% more time playing with their sons than with their daughters (Bunker, 1991). Their behavior during play is also different. For example, parents smile more at girls and encourage more active play from boys (Fagot, 1974).

Although boys and girls tend to play differently and to prefer different toys, the structure of the toy and the setting in which play occurs also elicit certain behaviors from players (Karpoe & Olney, 1983; Ross & Taylor, 1989). A Bobo doll, often used in aggression and toy research, invites punching, just as teddy bears invite cuddling. It is true that "boys will be boys," but it is also true that "footballs will be footballs" and "dolls will be dolls."

Social learning of play styles is not restricted to personal influence. It also involves mass media effects, such as the portrayal of boys and girls in toy packaging and advertising (Schwartz & Markham, 1985).

Sex roles in advertising

As early as age 3, heavy television viewers in the United States have more stereotyped views of sex roles than do light viewers. "Commercials are outstanding culprits in the presentation of sex role stereotypes," according to Greenfield (1984, p. 33).

Different techniques are used to promote toys for boys and girls. Commercials for girls' toys contain more fades, dissolves, and soft background music; those for boys' toys contain more action, frequent cuts, sound effects, and loud music. In a clever experiment, Greer, Potts, Wright and Huston (1982) created "pseudocommercials" for abstract shapes rather than for real products. Two types of commercial for abstract shapes were produced, one containing clusters of features that appeared mainly in advertisements for boys and one with features appearing in advertisements for girls. These pseudocommercials were shown to children. Children of all ages tended to identify the advertisements with girls' features as female and those with features from commercials for boys as male.

Kline and Pentecost (1990) observed "profound genderization" in 150 randomly selected commercials for toys from children's television. Children were shown in traditional sex roles. Doll play predominated among toy ads aimed exclusively at girls, accounting for 84% of these ads. Forty-five percent of boys' ads featured dolls, primarily ads for action figures. Boys were shown at play with a wider range of toys, including toy cars, guns, construction sets, and electronic video games. Despite the large number of doll ads in the sample, hardly any doll ads depict boys and girls playing together. Only a few ads (for stuffed animals) showed boys and girls playing together. Of the ads for dolls, 91% featured single-sex play groups, whereas 66% of nondoll play (e.g., games, cars, guns) showed single-sex groups. Games, on the other hand, which were about 10% of the sample, always showed boys and girls playing together.

Kline and Pentecost make the interesting observation that there is a difference in the way boys and girls are portrayed in relation to their toys. Girls are often shown *interacting* with their toys, that is, adopting a separate identity that interacts with that of the toy. Boys are most often shown *identifying* with toys, that is, taking on the character of the toy as their own. For example, in advertisements for My Little Pony, girls do not "become" ponies but rather assume identities or roles in relation to the ponies. When boys play Batman, they *become* Batman.

Toy advertising in Britain may be different. Seventy-five toy commercials shown on British television prior to Christmas 1988 were analyzed by Smith and Bennett (1990). The commercials were coded for sex-role stereotypes and aggression. There was exactly equal representation of males and females. Aside from dolls and toy cars, there were no sex differences for other products. Boys were more often shown in competitive play, whereas girls were shown in cooperative play. Boys were more active compared to girls. The most dramatic finding of the U.K. study was the overwhelming majority of male voice-overs: 74%.

There are clear differences, then, in the way toys are marketed to boys and girls. If Singer and Singer are correct in stating that the toy play of girls increasingly resembles that of boys, it is likely that advertising and packaging will come to reflect this changing reality.

Summary

Perceived differences between boys' and girls' play depends on who is doing the observing – man or woman, boy or girl; on their own experiences with the observed forms of play; and on their definitions of aggression. Despite the potential biases inherent in studies of children's play, there is widespread agreement that boys' play is far more physically aggressive than that of girls; and that compared with girls, boys prefer toy guns, adventure fantasy play, and video games with aggressive themes, whereas girls prefer household objects, enacting familiar roles, and dolls. These preferences develop early and appear to have biological as well as social origins. Of the latter, modeling by peers and parents seems to be especially potent.

Video and computer games, especially those with violent themes, appeal mainly to boys. Although some boys may be obsessed with video games, there is little evidence either that this is so or that video-game play is associated with social isolation, poor school performance, personality disorder, or excessive aggression. It may be a source of conflict in some families, however. Video game play is associated with improved cognitive skills, including attention, logical thinking, and hypothesis testing.

Sex differences in play and toy preference inevitably reflect sex differences in society in general. Because so much of children's play mimics adult behavior, it is unimaginable that the range of adult attitudes about sex roles would not be reflected in children's play and toy preferences.

7

Does play prepare the future?

BRIAN SUTTON-SMITH

It is possible to argue that there are two major kinds of rhetoric about play in this century. One says that play is a preparation for the future, the other that play is a form of adjustment to the present. We associate the *preparatory theory* with the Reformation, the Enlightenment, historicism, evolutionary theory, biology and developmental psychology, and more recently with feminism, and in all cases with its application to children. We associate the *adjustment theory* with Romanticism, with Freud, with phenomenology, and, most appropriately, with its application to adults, because it is hard to say that adults grow as a result of their play. Adults more often seem to be fixated in one place, incurably addicted to their pastimes. The preparatory view is optimistic; the adjustment view is probably pessimistic. There is always some hope for the young but not much for the old. The former view has to do with progress, the latter with contentment. Progress is a much harder master.

My Bundle Baby

In order to give some currency to this discussion of whether play prepares one for the future, I begin by focusing on a controversial toy that has just come onto the American market after being heralded at the international Toy Fair in New York in February 1992. The toy is a doll for 3- to 7-year-olds called My Bundle Baby. It is a typical spongy, soft doll, 11 inches tall. It comes enclosed in a soft bag with straps so that it can be hung on the back or on the front like the adult snuggly pack in which real babies are carried about. When you open the pack, you discover whether the stork (of which there is a picture inside) has brought you a boy or a girl, announced by the clothes the baby is wearing (pink or blue), as well as a tag saying "This is a girl" or "This is a boy." In addition, the doll can be used to simulate pregnancy, for when it is strapped on the front of the child and a small button on the bag is pushed by the wearer, the machine inside at the bottom of the bag makes noises and movements meant to represent the sound of a heart beating and feet kicking.

I have four married daughters and five granddaughters, so it seemed reasonable that I should see what they would do with it. A 2-year-old immediately stripped it of clothes and showed no further interest. A 3-year-old with a younger sibling was only interested in the machine that produced these noises and effects. She dragged it out, and we had to explain how it worked. Perhaps she was already too mature for it, as she had already had plenty of games of stuffing her own clothing into her own panties to simulate her mother's pregnant belly. A 4-year-old with a younger sister, however, became most attached to it and wore it on her back for several hours, becoming tearful when she had to give it up to go home. Several days later at her own house, she got hold of an elastic-type Ace bandage and wrapped it around her stomach so that she could fit her own baby doll into it and simulate pregnancy. She and her 2-year-old younger sister had already played many games of holding dolls under their dresses and bringing them out, head first, for "birthing." The 6-year-old was not much interested but kept the doll with her while she watched television. She had already played many games of stuffing Barbie doll clothes down Barbie's pants to simulate pregnancy for the svelte Barbie. In sum, these granddaughters of mine, who have multiple dolls and live in homes where there is open discussion of pregnancy and birthing, showed some curiosity and some willingness to play with the doll. Nothing exceptional took place.

Imagine, then, my surprise to read in *The New York Times* of February 6, 1992, a column by reporter Carol Lawson quoting many "experts" who were reacting in alarm to the idea of such a pregnancy plaything.[1] None of them, I might add, had seen it. There seemed to be three kinds of reaction:

1. that the doll was an invasion of parental rights and a violation of children's innocence;
2. that it was going to misinform the young about pregnancy; and
3. that it was going to create even more unwanted pregnancies in a country already suffering an epidemic of pregnancies in the very young. Let us consider these one at a time.

The invasion of parental rights

This point of view was expressed by the contemporary "dean" of American child care of the public airwaves, Dr. Terry Brazelton, who said, "The doll is a real invasion of the parent's opportunity to share something precious with a child. Who needs such a toy?" He was supported by Frances Stott, professor of early childhood development at the Erikson Institute in Chicago, who said that the toy was unnecessary and took away from the parents what they would do themselves. "When we talk to children about having babies we convey to them through our emotional tone the meaning of the experience," she said. Another correspondent called it a

[1] The statements here are derived largely from news sources following the appearance of the doll at the 1992 Toy Fair in New York. For example, see the articles by Carol Lawson, *The New York Times,* Feb. 6, 1992, page C1; Michelle Healy, *USA Today,* Feb. 5, 1992, p. 4D; editorial, *Washington Times,* Feb. 20, 1992; Leslie Baldacci, *Chicago Sun Times,* Mar. 15, 1992, p. 26; and Robin Abcarian, *Los Angeles Times,* Apr. 10, 1992. In addition, as a volunteer media referral person for the American Psychological Association, I receive calls from journalists on the issues of toys and play; these calls have also been a source of information.

most ridiculous product: "Let Mom deal with it. Who asked Mattel to play God?" And another said, "Let little girls have tea parties, pregnancy is no game."

Misinformation on pregnancy

A much larger group felt that the doll would give the child an anatomically incorrect version of reproduction. Thus, Debra Haffner, executive officer of the Sex Information and Education Council of the United States, said: "It is going to be very confusing to children. It will leave them with the idea that you can put on pregnancy and take it off when you want to... and that a fetus develops inside a pouch outside the body. The kids will think we are like Kangaroos." And David Elkind, professor of child development at Tufts University and famous replicator of Piagetian experiments in the United States, as well as author of *The Hurried Child,* said: "These toys are going too far. It is fine for little girls to play with dolls, but this one is far removed from what they can understand or appreciate. And what happens if it doesn't work? Is the baby dead?" (Quotes from Lawson, 1992; see footnote 1).

"They are terribly literal," says Joanne Oppenheim, author of the *Oppenheim Toy Portfolio,* a quarterly consumer guide. She goes on: "The doll is like the empathy belly for men, but do girls really need to know what it feels like to be pregnant at the age of four or five? What is left for children to imagine? Nothing surprises me. I think next year Barbie is going to get her period." Diana Huss Green, editor of the magazine *Parents Choice,* says: "Kids sound so wise when aping TV, magazines, newspapers. They know about and have got to know about condoms, drugs, wars, and other issues. But what do they really comprehend is the question?" Another correspondent says: "This is a warped perception... an abortion kit. Is pregnancy only feelings of kicking? Let children be children." Says another: "The stork brought it. That's hopelessly unreal. A fantasy view of pregnancy, a profusion of misunderstanding." Says still another: "I am appalled and disgusted

...it is sexist that all little girls should be mommies. It ignores teen pregnancies and women's rights. It reduces the critical issues to the level of fun and magical fantasies. It inappropriately emphasizes the importance of biological functions. It is a gross promotion of society's most limited assumptions about women. The manufacturers should refrain from making things worse."

Incitement to pregnancy

But the largest and most insistent voices in opposition belonged to those who felt that the doll was an incitement to more unwanted pregnancy. An editorial in the *Washington Times* (Feb. 20, 1992), says:

> There is something more than a little ironic about the glorification of pregnancy among three-year-olds in a society trying to curb the explosion of teenage pregnancies. The message delivered is: pregnancy is wonderful no matter what age you are. Unfortunately the kit says nothing about the rigors of parenthood. Very likely there was no room for that in the company's marketing strategy.

Most interesting is a manifesto released to the press in Cincinnati (Apr. 14, 1992) by a variety of signatories connected in one way or another with child pregnancy and including protagonists of the right-to-life (antiabortion) movement, along with protagonists of the right-to-choice (allowing abortion) movement, united here presumably for the first time in the history of their controversy, something fairly remarkable for a mere doll to effect. They say:

> The announcement by Mattel concerning the manufacturing and marketing of My Bundle Baby is of great concern to us who work daily with families who have experienced the premature pregnancy of a teenager, and subsequent teenage parenting. We believe that My Bundle Baby toy simulating a pregnancy sends

the wrong message to children and youth, conveying the idea that pregnancy is something to play with . . . that it is but a toy.

Mattel rebuts all of this by showing that in their surveys the majority of respondents (over 80%) did not find the idea of this toy or its purpose objectionable. What these antipathetical voices showed us is how profound is the belief among some educators and social workers in the United States that child play is a specific preparation for adult development. This is implied in all of the preceding quotations, disparate as they may be. All of these voices imply that what happens in play, down to the minute particulars of this doll, will have a great effect on the future of the players and of their country. Two assumptions seem involved. One involves specific *causality*. That is, the doll deprives the parents of their power, destroys the child's innocence, puts an end to imagination, misinforms children, and incites them to subsequent immoral behavior. Another assumption, perhaps prior to this one, is that the realistic features of the doll, as perceived by the adults speaking here, are also those that are perceived by and causative for the child. It sounds as if John Locke and his *tabula rasa* theory of perception have 300 years later become the common sense of both these experts and these ordinary folk.

As an aside, the much more specific Barbie-like European Judy doll, which has a belly that snaps off to reveal a baby and then is replaced with a flat tummy panel, is said to have caused no such explosion of concern in Europe, although it too has caused an eruption in this country. The two dolls, Bundle Baby and Judy, are being received as if they herald the end of family life. Perhaps, as Mencken says, all the Puritans came to America. Or is it that Europeans have not yet caught the same optimistic virus of human progress?

Play as preparation for the future

As mentioned earlier, the historical forces that predispose us to think about play in causal terms are immense. These include millennarian hopes of the Reformation. The panglossian expectation of eighteenth-century rationalists that the physical sciences could be replicated by the social sciences and human progress ensured. The growth of various kinds of historicism, like those of Hegel or Marx, which assumed that humanity could conceptualize human history as progressive and predictable. The evidence of evolution that the more complex species played in more complex ways and had longer periods of childhood in which such play could take place, so that play should be seen as an inevitable precursor of adult status. The growth of a science of childhood, which, following the metaphors of evolutionary theory, came to assume that childhood development occurred in predictable stages and, following the metaphors of the physical sciences, that it was also possible to find childrearing antecedents for later life outcomes. Although many of these beliefs, a great empire of optimism about predictable social progress, have largely gone down into the dust of secularism, holocausts, the decay of fascism and communism, the scientific production of bombs and pollution, as well as the empirical reality of the low-level scientific predictability of human behavior in general, the habit of thought still hangs on to maintain the illusion that such micro phenomena as Bundle Baby or Judy have detailed predictable consequences.

It seems also that children, and not just play, have become the residual legatees of this belief in historicism. Children have become, as it were, the last guarantors of our progress; therefore, we must find and make predictable the future that they will have for us. We concede them the future and then organize them to guarantee that it will be the one we wish to see. All of the commentators on Bundle Baby seem unaware that these immodest epistemological claims for historical and individual predictability are now largely forfeit (Sutton-Smith, in press).

There are, however, several other practical effects of this naive realism. The continuance of this mythology of predictability allows us skeptics to guess how the future might be prepared for play by the rhetorics of these very predictors themselves. Note not how play shapes the future, but how these people who think you can predict detailed outcomes in our twentieth-century culture will continue to attempt to arrange the future of children's play. There is a difference, I would claim, between trying to predict an individual outcome over 20 years from a unique childhood toy event and trying to predict that cultural habits with a long history will probably continue. Some of these historical events that suggest the future of toys and play follow.

The domestication of childhood

The major play event of the past 300 years has been the ever-increasing domestication of children's play (Sutton-Smith, 1986). By that I mean the increasing control and supervision of play to get rid of its physical dangers and its emotional licenses. This has been accomplished by innumerable cultural agencies such as schools' playground supervision; physical education; sports organizations for ever-younger players; recreational organizations (such as the Boy Scouts and other groups); and, more recently in the United States, in some cases, by the abolition of playtime; the discouragement of play fighting and war toys and the encouragement of bisexual play and bisexual toys; the encouragement of teacher–child play, therapist–child play, and parent–child play; and the encouragement of curriculum play inside schools. To what extent these developments are a result of this ideology of the child as the future, or more simply just one more facet of the increasingly coherent regulation of the nation-state, to follow the scholarly suggestions of either Foucault (1973) or Elias (1982) remains uncertain.

What does seem likely is that we can predict more of the same organization of forms of public play in the future. For example, we would expect the continued and increasing organization of children's behavior in summer camps, day camps, and church camps. There seems no reason to imagine that all of the arts and sports organizations will not continue to proselytize at younger and younger age levels. In the 1960s, the trend toward interactive children's museums (or learning centers) began; there are now more than 200 in the United States, with such names as Please Touch Museum, Imaginarium, Exploratorium, Discovery, Kidspace, Insect Zoos, and Cowboy Town. Most of the older museums have, in turn, developed new provisions for children. The development of adventure lands and fantasy lands, planetariums, and aquariums has also grown apace; and we seem now on the threshold of an era when play centers like the Sesame Street center in Pennsylvania may become a part of most department stores, even perhaps in every McDonalds. We may also be on the verge of moving beyond video game arcades for adolescents into the kinds of structured war games now played in large indoor spaces by adults. Nor is it improbable that some of the outdoor summer organizations will likewise stage these paint-shooting games for their clientele. I well remember my own YMCA summer camp experience of 1934, where two teams played "capture the flag" across a half mile of wild rural terrain in Foxton, New Zealand. All we had to fire with was straw inside a paper bag, though some of us added cow dung to beef (*sic*) up the weight and power of the projectile. Nothing changes but the gloss.

The toy makers, for their part, are beginning to talk of an Annual Toy Festival giving children a midyear chance to play with new toys and prototype toys in the 10 major cities, perhaps linked to the availability of some of these in the adjacent Toys R Us stores. On the horizon is the more organized use of commercial toys throughout elementary education schoolrooms, a technique recently pioneered by Waltraut Hartmann in Vienna and found to be highly reinforcing for other kinds of school interest and progress. In general, what we are seeing is the beginning of the kind of "commodification" of childhood that has been used with adolescents throughout the century. Once any demographic group has money to spend, the usual commercial agencies direct their advertising in that direction and begin to affect the fashions and enthusiasms of the target group. This has been happening with children for the past 20 years. Barbies, GI Joes, and particularly the Cabbage Patch dolls were remarkable for becoming "fashions" that appealed for periods of time to millions of children. Television advertising, in association with children's programming, has made the public of childhood aware of its possibilities. Toys, music, clothing, candy, and food are now focused directly at this market group, contributing to the imaginative play in their lives. Undoubtedly some of the antagonism to the Bundle Baby's invasion of family life has been instigated by the fact that it is one more representation of this larger trend toward childhood commodification, against which there has been a rearguard upper status, highly educated reaction for centuries. Mass recreations have never been favored by those who have money, talent, or taste for more highly differentiated pursuits. In addition to the domestication of childhood, there has been what we might lamentably neologize as the domestication of play.

The domestication of play

A predominant facet of the domestication of modern childhood play is its movement *indoors*. Whereas our mothers used to say, "Don't bother me, go and play outside," often they no longer make that suggestion because they feel that the streets are unsafe or that their companions are undesirable. Instead they take their children to some of the public organizations or places already mentioned. Or they may import more carefully selected playmates, or banish their children to the family playroom (or basement) or to their bedrooms, festooned with the commodities of childhood. Or they may simply say, "Go and watch television." This means that the home has become increasingly the major play space for children, as well as adults. No one would have considered such a thing possible in past centuries. Given television, more time is spent in private play space than in public play space. Indoor play is used to exercise the privacy and subjectivity of children and adults as it never has been before.

What has happened to the home is that much of the children's furniture once found only in creative preschool settings now is found there. There are suitable chairs and tables, and in the back yard there are plastic pools, swings, slides, tents, and picnic tables, all child-sized. We may expect in the future, given the current trends towards child obesity and lack of physical fitness, that features of adult health spas and sports bars will also come to be found in the home. Perhaps with the television high on the wall, the erstwhile television room, recreation room, or basement will feature Nordic Tracks, weight-lifting apparatus, and stationary bicycles. The more certain part of the play apparatus of the future, however, will center on the computer screen and will probably be kept in the bedroom, where various kinds of highly privatized reality – virtual or otherwise – will be available to the child. One can obviously expect a vast increase in modern linked groups with particular interests – most obviously, the members of the same school-focused interests during spare time. A great deal of this already happens in an informal way between children who can mutually create stories, dramas, poems, and letters on their linked computers.

In an unpublished study of mine comparing 9-year-old New Zealand children's play between 1950 and 1990, this was one of the major differences in their imaginative activity. In 1950 they talked of their cowboys and Indians games; in 1990 they talked of making up theater plays together on their computers. But perhaps more exciting, some of the adult computer-connected circuits of today (such as Fantasy Baseball and Rotisserie Baseball, in which the players are randomly allocated real baseball players and their own game fate depends on the actual performances and scores of those players) will be made feasible at the child level. Interactive video certainly implies that most adult games – Jeopardy, Trivial Pursuit, Dungeons and Dragons – will ultimately have their modern computer counterparts at the child level.

The generational law of play is that adult pursuits that can pass the domestication value threshold will sink down to more childish levels. This is also apparently an anthropological law: It is often easier to grasp another culture through the games it plays than through its supposedly more realistic features. Children likewise reach up for the caricatures provided by adult recreations.

The solitariness of childhood

In my book *Toys as Culture* (1986), I wrote about the solitariness of childhood in the twentieth century. Throughout most of history, play has been social, collective, and public. Now we have an increasingly extensive form of private, personal, or solitary play largely devoted to common or unique fantasies. This is a remarkable shift in the cultural evolution of play in our time. The history of toys is in part a history of the evolution of those objects that are to be played with individually. Interestingly, even the theories of child play in this century, from Freud to Piaget, are largely about solitary players. Most modern psychological explanations of play are in terms of processes ascribed to the individual player, his or her motivations, cognitions, or pleasures. When anthropologists and historians look at their adult subjects in their collective festivals and sports, however, their explanations are quite different and refer to cultural events such as mass inversions of power, gender, race, and age. They do not, in general, highlight individual passions or processes.

Toys as gifts and bonds

At the same time that toys and play have moved inside, the toys are not only expected to be played with by the child personally, they are also given as part of family bonding. The majority of toys are given as gifts. In effect, the parent says, "I give you this gift to bond you to me; now go and play with it by yourself." Solitariness often means loneliness, so some of these gifts are soft toys, animals, and dolls, which the child will treat as imaginary companions. In fact, all toys can be seen as a bridge between one's own emotional life and the more objective world outside. That outside world can be represented in doll play as dealing with caretaking, or in video-game play as occupied with war games, or in building and science-based toys as representing the technological object world in which we all live and to which we must adapt.

Toys also sustain gender bonding despite efforts to advocate a new order between the genders. It has been maintained that such bonding is more rigid in group play than anywhere else and that, hence, this is one reason for the lack of success in selling toys across gender lines.

What these generalizations accomplish is to suggest the paradoxical ways in which toys contribute to our modern domestic and gender identities, as well as to our capacities for solitary persistence and concentration. Toys as safe play in the home nurture the private individual while paradoxically developing those individual competencies most essential for success in the public arena.

The sanitization of vulgarity

As we look at the future of toys in terms of the future for which they prepare us, we would have to say, on the basis of the record presented here, that we seem to be conditioned to more civilized social play and more fantastic solitary play than were characteristic of earlier centuries.

Despite all the mythology about the child being the future and play preparing us for the future, the main purpose of toys seems to be to keep us civilized and in good taste, no matter what we are doing. One notes the ever-increasing antiseptic "grossness" on television for children, particularly on the only channel for children, Nickelodeon, where there is a clear antiparent bias and where children and parents compete with each other in throwing rubbish and slime, falling into water, and so on. This new sublimation of vulgarity is still too much for some. In Cincinnati there is a report of a group called Citizens for the Prevention of Mental Pollution that has come out against such programs as *The Simpsons,* the child cartoon *Rem,* and *Stimpy,* and the production of toys that personify vomit or snot, as well as television programs that include farting and references to body functions in general.

Play as a form of adjustment

To this point, I have placed the rhetoric of play as preparation within larger historical trends within Western society, and that may be all there is to it. Most of us have also assumed that there is a grounding for these expectations of play in biology and possibly in psychology. But there appears to be some confusion about their meaning.

For example, it is easy to assume that a behavior as ubiquitous in humans, mammals, and birds as play must have some evolutionary function, particularly as the amount of play across these species is correlated with the size of the brain. Again, because play is so widespread in such different species, its function in solving adaptational problems must also be of a very general kind. However, in animals as in humans, direct learning via exploration or imitation is not the same as the highly repetitive mimicry and mockery of normative behavior that characterize play. Play may have been in the first place an imitative reproduction of adaptive behavior inappropriately, behavior that had the immediate effect of not being a fatal mistake because it was produced out of its real context (Hattiengadi, 1987). For example, rough-and-tumble play presumably was selected for at some point in evolution as a way of establishing hierarchies without fatal injury. The difference between such exploratory learning, common to all life forms, and play, common only to higher forms, is like the difference between tools and toys. Tools have clear-cut, practical usage and consequences. Toys do not. They are turned paradoxically in on themselves. Thus a toy doll like Bundle Baby is not a baby. Or to put it in current Wayne parlance, it is a baby. NOT. It has flesh. NOT. It has skin. NOT. It talks, speaks, acts, feels. NOT. Which is a nice version of the earlier Bateson statement that the baby doll is not a real baby, but neither is it not not a baby (Bateson, 1972). From all of this, we can see that toys are an early lesson in deconstructive thought. The toy is often a representation that, because of its miniaturism, gigantism, schematism, or caricature, immediately denies its own representation of reality, pronouncing itself ready instead for a reaction of fantasy or phantasmagoria. Unfortunately, some adults in states of high anxiety about sex, material culture, or moral responsibility do not perceive the paradox. They act with what the famous nineteenth-century anthropologist James G. Frazer (1949) called *sympathetic magic,* saying that the slight likeness between pregnant dolls and pregnant unmarried mothers is a sufficient cause. That is, the first, the doll, causes the second, the pregnancy. It is a conceptual process somewhat on a par with sticking pins in effigies to kill those they are said to represent.

What is characteristic of our knowledge of animal play is that the lack of play signifies stress; in humans the lack of play also typically signifies mental illness, depression, or social maladjustment. The presence of play is more often associated with general vitality, with physical and mental health. This leads to the assertion that play has more to do directly with emotional adjustment than it has to do with the acquisition of knowledge, although the latter can be an indirect result of the higher levels of general motivation instigated by opportunities to play. The fact that the two, exploration and play, are often observed together suggests, in turn, that they operate in tangent to make some kind of dialectical sense. After all, you can toy with tools or tool with toys. It has often been said that there is probably a functional relationship between the receptivity of exploration and the assertiveness of play. The one gives dominance to the world and the other to the organism. The one is about external epistemic events, and the other is about personal ontological events; the one is about learning something, and the other is about pretending to be in charge of the something that has been learned. There is an oscillation between the two. One might say paradoxically, of play's more assertive and less receptive role, that it is the place to pretend that life is worth living.

Put in these terms, play becomes more like night or day dreaming than like problem solving. It is an autogenous function that brings the organism, by its own asserted virtual actions, back into a state of some equilibrium with its own received understandings. It is perhaps no accident that children will usually play at those external events that they most worry about, fear, or hate. George Eisen's work "Children and play in the holocaust" (1988) is a telling example. But even children's mundane play at house and at war reflect their two greatest gender anxieties: to be able to give birth to or manage babies and to be able to fight and die. Is it any more surprising that animal games are mainly about fighting, chasing, and escaping? Perhaps animals also need to summon up their confidence in the midst of their explorations of their particular competencies.

This kind of rhetoric, which we might associate with Freud and Erikson rather than with Berlyne and Piaget, seems to me contrary to the cognitive trend of the past 30 years. Anthropological theories of play, as found in carnivals, festivals, and sports, and emphasizing the world turned upside down in these events, also speak to the feelings of their audiences that they can overcome, even if only in fantasy. What children and adults have in common in their quite different kinds of play, in this view, is their need for empowerment in a world that largely disempowers them. The children are disempowered by adults and by their own weakness, and the adults are disempowered either by their gods or their perceptions of mortality. The play of both is a temporary cry of triumph.

Which is to say that the little girls with their Bundle Babies or any of their other hundreds of dolls are busy persuading themselves that they also can overcome their contemporary infantile anxieties about these events, about having and maintaining babies. In these terms, toys are meant for the empowerment of play rather than as teaching machines that can replace what parents want their children to learn. But I suppose that parents who don't want their children to learn anything at all about sex, or don't want them to learn anything at all about sex from anyone or anything else but themselves, are bound to be cast into self-deluding anxiety by the invasion of these new agents of play or information. The argument of this chapter is that if play prepares the future, it is by creating more vigorous, active children who find in their play a dream of confidence that they can also manage their fate.

As a final note, I must call puzzled attention to the great disjunction between adults and children in this culture that makes us think that play is what children do but not what adults do. This disjunction apparently permits us to attempt to control and domesticate children's play on behalf of their future. We rationalize our own quite irrational play behavior by calling it only entertainment, and we then prevent children from exhibiting such irrationality by saying that they will grow through their play if we keep it sanitized. We can play irrationally (our games of chance are a $250 billion dollar industry, about the same as the military budget), but they must not. By making play a rational series of steps and stairs toward wisdom and understanding, we keep them under our control, and we keep out of their lives any of those elements of common human irrationality that make us uncomfortable about our own systems of belief, morality, and sexuality. In these systems of belief, it is not that play prepares the future; it is rather that play, or control of it, guarantees that we can control the future of our children on our own rather narrow behalf.

So I urge people that when they accept the rhetoric that play prepares the future, they ask themselves who is playing here, who is kidding whom. Children need their play to make the present tolerable to themselves, and to do that they need a lot of time to themselves. We should defend that need and not intrude upon it for the protection of our own past values under the guise of preparing their future.

8
Play as healing

DOROTHY G. SINGER

Introduction

Jean Piaget, the psychologist, asked, "Why indeed does the child play at being a shopkeeper, a driver, a doctor?" He believed that a child formed a "vast network of devices which allow the ego to assimilate the whole of reality, i.e., to integrate it in order to re-live it, to dominate it or to compensate. Even games with dolls, which might lend themselves to a special interpretation, are much less pre-exercise of the maternal instinct than an infinitely varied symbolic system which provides the child with all the means of assimilation it needs in order to rethink past experiences" (1962).

The children I work with not only relive their past experiences through play but also try to work out current conflicts that relate to themselves or to their caregivers. Just as Piaget observed his own children trying to "liquidate" disagreeable situations by re-living them in their make-believe play, I too believe that play can be healing.

Parents often ask, "What is play therapy?" They want to know how play can lead to growth and how it can help ease the pain their child is experiencing. I think it is important to make a distinction between "just playing" and play therapy. The therapist adopts a particular orientation or strategy that may include a variety of treatment approaches, depending on the nature of the child's disturbance, temperament, and age. But irrespective of any particular approach, the play therapist's goal is to help children gain a positive self-concept, master conflicts and anxieties, and develop competence in dealing with incidents that they may never truly experience within the playroom. A child, for example, may be terrified of the dark and have trouble falling asleep. This exact situation obviously will not occur in the playroom, but through play therapy the child will learn how to cope with fears in general; eventually, he or she will conquer that fear at home.

Some children who come to my playroom do not know how to play and seem to have difficulty using their imagination. They have missed the delight and fun of play or what is sometimes referred to as the *flow*. This flow occurs when action and awareness merge, enabling children to become less self-conscious and less aware of their own body states (Csikszentmihalyi, 1976). These children, the nonplayers, will be guided by me, step by step, as I interact with them, first, in simple play and then by gradually introducing more materials or ideas for make-believe games (Singer, 1993). I tread slowly and carefully, allowing the child (if he or she wishes or can) to take the lead, to initially choose the materials or games preferred. Subtly, I try to shape the child's behavior to become more constructive, or more restricted if the play is aggressive and wild, but always attempting to give the child a sense of control, accomplishment, and what Kevin O'Connor calls "joyous abandon" (1991).

Children use symbolism when they play. Through internal representations of reality, a child seeks to imitate and accommodate to complex adult actions and speech. Gradually, externally generated material is reshaped and assimilated in novel ways into the child's existing memory schemas. When this occurs, games become more elaborate and complex. Children develop scripts so that pretend play has some order and meaning for them (Singer & Singer, 1990). An onlooker may wonder what a particular block construction signifies, or why dolls are placed in a cardboard box or in a "cave" made out of pillows and an upturned chair. The child has an image or plan in mind, a story that allows a game to be sustained with a beginning, middle, and ending. Through careful observation of a child's play configurations, and through listening to a child's conversations, I am able to make interpretations about his or her emotional state.

My approach is eclectic but based on humanist play therapy, a model developed by Carl Rogers and adapted by Virginia Axline and Clark Moustakis, pioneers in the field of play therapy. Within this tradition, my goal is to create a play environment that is positively reinforcing. I do this by responding empathically, by respecting the child, by interacting with the child through words and play, by setting clear, realistic limits, and by building trust between the child and myself. Trust develops by accepting the child as he or she is. I try not to be impatient or to hurry a child. If there is a need for silence, that is supported. If there is a need to repeat a pretend game, that is also accepted, allowing the child to work through feelings as the game is played many times. I listen carefully and encourage a child to express feelings. I reflect on those feelings. Through this process, children begin to gain insight into their behavior. I try to be flexible. Within the humanist therapy model, I may at times use a particular technique that I believe will be suitable for a specific problem. I use (1) *traditional play techniques:* doll house, dress-up clothes, puppets, water play, arts and crafts materials, blocks, miniature figures, cars, trucks, board games, and music; (2) *modeling behavior through role playing:* the child and I take turns becoming a sibling, parent, or teacher, for example, thus enabling the child to imitate more appropriate responses in conflict situations; (3) *imagery techniques:* a child is encouraged, without the use of props, to picture people and events and to experience moods, conflicts, and resolutions in the mind; and (4) *behavior modification:* a child's positive behaviors are reinforced through external rewards such as a star and a sticker, leading ultimately to self-reward or intrinsic satisfaction.

Parents play a vital role in the play therapy process. I deem it essential that parents attend a monthly session with me, where I then share my concerns about the child, listen to their concerns as well, and make recommendations that will hopefully alter child-rearing patterns that may not have been beneficial. The school, whether a preschool or an elementary school, is another facet in the mending process. Meetings with school personnel and observations of the child in the classroom are necessary to gain a clearer picture of the social and emotional development of each client. Finally, I meet regularly with a small group of other psychologists who specialize in working with young children. We present our cases, share ideas about new assessment and treatment methods, share books and pamphlets – any material that we believe will stimulate our own thinking. We also share material that we feel would be appropriate for parents to read. Thus, working with children is a time-consuming profession, but one that offers many gratifications. Children are flexible, responsive to a caring adult, and eager to rid themselves of their problems; as one child has said to me, "I want the boo-boos in my mind to go away."

The playroom

There are certain basic elements that I believe are necessary in a playroom. Space, of course, is important so that a child will not feel confined. However, a room that is too large may make a child feel lost and distant from the therapist. I am fortunate to have two areas that can be separated by a wooden blind. This allows a smaller, cozy room that provides security for some children; alternatively, the blind can be raised, affording a larger space if I want to work with groups. There is a carpeted area in both rooms, so that we can sit on the floor for quiet activities or for play that may be a bit more rough. Part of the room has tile on the floor, which is fine for water or paint spills, or for riding a small vehicle or running miniature-car races. There is a bathroom adjoining the playroom, essential when working with young children. It was a crucial element in working with Robert, a child I will discuss who had a toilet phobia.

There is a large sliding-glass door at one end of the playroom. It can be covered by drapes or, if necessary, the drapes can be opened so that a child can see the garden and feel less confined.

The glass is tempered, double pane. It is essential that windows or doors, if made of glass, be shatterproof. A child I worked with had a habit of quickly picking up a block or car and hurling it across the room toward the glass when he was angry. Needless to say, this behavior was one of the first elements I tackled in play therapy with him.

Equipment should be simple. I have a work table and chairs for board games, arts and crafts, and writing stories. There is also a small table and chairs for tea parties, birthday parties, and playing restaurant, or store, Several cabinets contain toys that are not on display and for keeping and storing toys that we do play with. I also have a couch in the room in case a child wants to play bed time or just cuddle with a soft toy. There is also a comfortable armchair for a child to sit in and relax whenever I use imagery techniques. A small slide in one corner of the room also has a boxlike place under the platform. This makes a good "house" for dolls, a "cave" for pirates, or even a hiding place for a small child. A boy I worked with years ago used this "nest" for retreat when-ever he needed to have a quiet moment to think. Generally, he crawled into this space after he had exploded in rage. Here he would recover, come out, and feel "new" again.

Play materials are rather standard in most playrooms. If one uses a more psychoanalytic approach, the toys are apt to be those that have particular significance for the child – doll houses with parent and sibling figures, stuffed animals, and some arts and crafts materials. Those of us who are eclectic tend to have a variety of toys that make our playrooms resemble a well-stocked room in a nursery school. Some therapists believe that a playroom should be relatively bare so that the child will be forced to interact more with the therapist than with the toys. In my experience, if there is a variety of toys, a child will find something he or she likes; then, using that choice, the therapist has the opportunity to engage the child. Most children (especially preschoolers) do not readily verb-alize their problems, but as they play and become more relaxed, the therapist finds a way to root out what may be causing the child emotional pain.

I consider essential equipment to be the following: a sturdy wooden doll house with family figures that are pliable so that they can sit, bend, and move the arms and legs. Dolls of both sexes are desirable. I have several large dolls that became the "friends" and even "enemies" of my clients. I also have two anatomically correct dolls for use with children who have been sexually abused. A baby doll that can be bathed is useful. Props such as baby bottles, baby blankets, and small plastic tubs or "shoe box beds" are always in use. Dishes, plastic utensils, and pots and pans for cooking become the major props when we play house or restaurant. Telephones, doctor kits, or a small tool box can be used in many pretend games. A rack of dress-up clothes and a bag of hats provide a child with the impetus to be a police officer, fire fighter, car driver, astronaut, cowboy, or cowgirl, train engineer or mother or father going to work. I keep a large blanket in the room; when it is placed over the table, it makes a wonderful tent, pirate cave, secret clubhouse, or even an animal's den. The array of soft stuffed animals often join a child in this safe, snug place and offer a child protection from the dark or "wild beasts" or "monsters."

Miniature figures such as pirates, space people, family figures, astronauts, and even animals are useful when we build structures out of blocks. The child can manipulate these figures and change voices. Through whatever pretend game he or she chooses, I can see a personal dilemma unfold before my eyes. As children play, I can offer alternatives for settling the conflict or struggles they are experiencing. Through the miniaturized play, the child makes sense out of a confusing larger world and, through my comments, relates these events to his or her personal life.

Markers, water colors, crayons, Play Doh, pipe cleaners, construction paper, large drawing pads, feathers, buttons, and corks can all be used to make objects and to release feelings. Records, audiotapes, and books are also in the playroom. Some children need to move with the music, learn how to relax, and become less stiff or self-conscious. Reading a story together about an animal who is afraid and then manages to take a risk helps a child cope with personal terrors. Puppets and a small puppet theater have been particularly useful in my work. A child who was unable to tell me about her fear of ceiling fans used puppets and enacted a playlet wherein puppets would not go into the airplane "because the propeller whirled." Gradually, she was able to verbalize her own fear, and through continued puppet play and desensitization techniques, she eventually overcame this phobia.

Board games, specifically checkers, are desirable with older children. Playing checkers enables a child to learn how to take turns, to cooperate, and to win and lose with grace. Because of the structure of the game and the competition involved, a child can generalize from this game to other forms of social play with peers that involve similar prosocial behaviors.

There is always ample opportunity during sessions for a child to just talk and not play. And this does happen. Sometimes a child bonds very quickly and feels trusting enough, or has enough insight about a particular problem, or is so concerned about a fear that verbalization needs little prompting on my part. Some children need to work with their hands, and as they draw or construct an object, they become more relaxed, more willing to share a burden. Sometimes an art rendition is quite explicit and suggestive of anxiety. But I try to be cautious; sometimes my probe or interpretation will lead to withdrawal or resistance until the child is more comfortable with me and ready to reveal some feelings and attitudes. Aaron Esman describes a child who was playing with cowboys and Indians. He flung them around the room wildly.

> To have suggested that it appeared that he was expressing his rage against his rigid punitive parents would, at this early stage of treatment, have induced either bland denial or angry resistance. The principal aim of the moment was to connect the action with a named affect...therapeutic tact – and tactics – dictated, then, the comment, "that cowboy sure looks angry at those Indians." "Sure he is," said Peter. "They keep taking his things away from him." (1983, p. 15)

Later, Peter was able to relate his rage and anger to his parents.

Case 1 – bereavement: the use of traditional play materials

The first case I present utilized a traditional play therapy approach but incorporated modified Rogerian principles. I permitted the child, Lois Melton, to choose her toys and games.[1] As she played, I responded with empathy both to the feelings expressed and to the actions she initiated with the toys. I also did some role playing to help her modify her interactions with her father. As with all of my clients, I set limits and provided structure in terms of how often and how long our sessions would be. Through Lois's symbolic play and use of her imagination, I was able to see her worries unfold. Play was also restorative for her. As she gained strength and saw other possibilities for herself, despair began to fade, and Lois became more optimistic about her future.

Lois's mother, Jean, was dying of cancer. This 8-year-old child needed to work through her feelings about her impending loss and the adjustment she would have to make after Mrs. Melton's death. Her parents were divorced. Her father, Ron, had remarried and would have legal custody of Lois on her mother's death. On occasion, Lois visited her father's home in a different state and spent long periods during holidays and summer vacations with him and his new family. My goals were to help Lois accept, as best she could, the knowledge that her mother was dying and that she would be uprooted from school, from her home, and from her friends. Lois was caught between two parents who had experienced a miserable marriage and an ugly divorce, and who now barely communicated with each other. They were in continual struggle over decisions concerning the legal and physical custody of Lois. Jean clearly did not want Ron to have Lois after her death but found, to her distress, that as the biological father and clearly not a felon, Ron Melton would indeed be granted custody of Lois.

[1]The names of clients and their families have been changed to preserve confidentiality.

When Lois came for therapy, she was resistant to the process, maintaining distance through the use of word games and puzzles. She invented "secret codes" that she offered to me to decipher. Her defenses were intellectual; she engaged me in these games, trying to decide whether or not she could trust me. Denial was another defense that Lois used, insisting that "Mommy was okay" and that she, Lois would "never, never live with Daddy." I was working against time; it wasn't clear how long Jean would have to live. She had tried various treatments, spent time in and out of hospitals, and was willing to act as a guinea pig, trying new drugs. Just as Jean fought against her illness, Lois resisted accepting the gradual deterioration of her physical and psychological strength.

Lois is a pretty child with long blonde hair, blue eyes, and dimples that give her face an impish expression when she smiles. Smiling, however, was rare during our first encounters. She was serious, quiet, and distant. In order to impress me, Lois brought me her school test papers so that I would admire her perfect scores. This was Lois's way of making contact with me on an intellectual level. She carefully avoided any questions I asked about her family and insisted that we "stick to our puzzles." She evidenced great pleasure when she beat me in a word game.

Me: "You like to win."
Lois: "Yes, I sure do. I feel awful whenever I lose a game."
Me: "Why?"
Lois: "I don't know – it's like I'm no good or dumb."
Me: "Do you think you always have to win?"
Lois: "Well, no, but losing is bad or scary."
Me: "Scary?"
Lois: "Yes. Don't lose anything, that's my rule!"
Me: "Grownups lose games, and even very smart people lose games. We can't always win."
Lois: "Well, you have to – that's all."

Me: "Why?"

Lois: "I don't know. Anyway, I don't want to talk about this!"

Lois was afraid of loss – loss of her mother, loss of her security. It was important for her to hold tightly to whatever she had, and games were symbols for her family. However, after a month of our word games and puzzle play, Lois felt more comfortable with me and began to explore the playroom. She took the doctor's kit from the cabinet and began to play with a small bear, examining it as she played doctor.

Lois: "I don't like to be sick, and I don't want anyone to be sick."

Me: "Who's sick, Lois?"

Lois: "No one – let's play house."

Lois did play house during our next sessions. She cuddled the dolls and the bear and fed them, play-acting "mother," but when I attempted to comment on this tenderness, Lois retreated and made it clear that she did not want to talk about her mother. Her play was focused on dealing with the mothering that she so sorely needed and feared that she would lose. At about this time, approximately 2 months after therapy had begun, Jean's condition worsened considerably, and Lois's play reflected this situation. Lois began to build what looked like a closed box.

Me: "You're making something, I see."

Lois: "It's a tower. I'm playing princess. Here she is inside. There are no windows, no doors. No one can come in. No one can go out."

Me: "It seems like that princess wants to be alone."

Lois: "Yes, she's safe here. She's protected. This is a palace all around here. Here is a mother, a father, one brother, a husband, a maid. People can come into the palace – but only four at a time."

Me: "The princess never leaves the tower."
Lois: "No, never. She needs to stay in there always."
Me: "Always is a long time. When will she come out?"
Lois: "She might go out, but in disguise – maybe on a
          picnic. Everyone is in the palace. All the people are
          there to protect her, to keep her safe. She is afraid to
          go out."

The princess in the tower was Lois's game throughout the next month. Her play symbolized her fear of being alone after Jean's death. What Lois could not tell me in words directly, she told me through this game. Lois saw herself surrounded by people she loved but isolated from them in her tower. Her play theme was one of security and protection. Only in her tower, where there were no windows, no doors, was she safe. She did not have to cope with her mother's death or be separated from her. Lois played this game while her mother fought valiantly to recover.

A few sessions later, as our relationship developed, Lois seemed ready to accept some suggestions that I had made. Perhaps the princess could open a window and look out. Perhaps she could visit a family in the doll house, where it was safe, and see if she liked it there. Lois sucked her thumb, came over to me and sat on my lap, and seemed to be giving these ideas some thought. She looked at me and didn't reply, but I felt that she had recognized what she was doing in her princess game. She became very quiet and then told me that we could play house. She went to the tower and removed some blocks, leaving an opening for a door and windows, but the princess doll remained inside. Over the next few sessions, the princess doll "watched" as Lois played with a favorite doll, a "momma doll" who tenderly fed her babies and tucked them into their beds. We began to make some progress: The princess could look out the window; the door was open, and Lois played family. Her thoughts were slowly turning toward her new family. Her father had two children with his second wife, and this would be Lois's new home. The fear of being alone and abandoned had lessened. Lois wanted a loving mother and security. She began to think about Ron Melton's new family as hers, but she still had not truly accepted this situation. To do so signified the final end of Jean's life, and in Lois's mind, this acceptance would be a betrayal of Jean.

As the months wore on, Lois was able to talk more openly about death, loneliness, and her new life to be. One day, Lois knocked the tower down, allowed the princess to come out, and never played that game again.

Jean Melton died approximately 8 months after therapy had begun. Lois grieved, but play therapy allowed her to deal with her great pain and eventual loss. The images in Lois's mind became miniaturized games that she could control, even though she could not control or prevent Jean's death. Lois's final games with me focused on a toy swan:

Lois: "Look. A newborn bird will come out of this shell. We will have a magic potion and make a baby mouse too."

Me: "You want some babies around, I see."

Lois: "This will be a game where a witch comes to these dolls – Lulu, Doo-Doo, Pooh-Pooh – and makes all new babies."

Me: "So many new babies."

Lois: "Well, it's new – beginning."

Lois then picked up two sets of parent dolls and placed them in the doll house. "Both families can live there now. Everyone goes to sleep. They all live together."

Lois did go to live with her father. I heard from her after she moved. She continued in therapy. I hope that Lois's native intelligence, her capacity for insight, and her gift of imagination will help keep the princess free from the tower forever.

Case 2 – a toilet phobia: desensitization, behavior modification, and art as therapy techniques

The reviews in the research literature on the outcome of psycho-therapy with adults and children generally support the efficacy of treatment (Casey & Berman, 1985; Smith, Glass & Miller, 1980). Casey and Berman found that in the 75 studies they examined, treated children achieved outcomes about two-thirds of a standard deviation better than those achieved by untreated children. Be-havioral methods appeared to be more effective than other forms of treatment, but this result, they claimed, was due to the types of outcome and target problems included in the behavioral studies.

The case in which I used desensitization and a behavior mod-ification technique involved a 6-year-old child, Robert Fraser, who had a toilet phobia. It began when his parents installed a swimming pool in their yard. Robert noticed the filter and was convinced that he would be sucked down the drain. That day he refused to go to the toilet and urinated in the wooded area behind the house. For 4 days he did this and became constipated, refusing to have a bowel movement. The Frasers finally convinced Robert to use one toilet in their home by covering the hole with toilet paper. Robert was still afraid but complied. This was the only toilet he would use. This incident occurred when Robert was 5, approxi-mately a year before he entered treatment. During that year, Rob-ert, who was in kindergarten, refused to use the school toilet and would not use toilets in restaurants or in the homes of relatives or friends. If the family dined out, they had to leave a restaurant, even if the meal was unfinished, and drive home; then Robert would use that toilet.

The family was in distress. Robert controlled their lives to the extent that they no longer dined out, canceled a vacation because a motel bathroom frightened him, and only visited their immediate family for short periods of time. Robert has a brother 1 year younger who teased him and exacerbated Robert's problem.

Grandparents cajoled Robert to use their bathrooms, offering all kinds of bribes, but to no avail. The Frasers were angry and frustrated and still did not recognize the need for professional help. They kept thinking that this was a phase. Robert would outgrow it; this was just an exaggeration of a normal stage.

Finally, a month before I met the Frasers, Robert had his yearly physical exam with a pediatrician. Robert refused to go to the toilet to give a urine sample. He "went crazy," according to his mother, and a full-blown tantrum with kicking, screaming, and flailing of the arms and legs ensued. The pediatrician wisely suggested psychotherapy; hence the referral to me.

Robert is a handsome, dark-haired, brown-eyed 6-year-old who, despite this phobia, relates well. He is receptive to people, polite, articulate, and intelligent. At our first meeting, he asked if I would "force" him to go to the toilet. When I reassured him that I would not, he seemed more relaxed and was able to tell me that "toilets bother me." My plan was to ignore the toilet situation until rapport was firmly established and I could sense that Robert trusted me. I discovered that Robert's favorite toys were Bigfoot trucks and "any kind of car or truck." We played with cars and trucks on the floor, building garages, warehouses, filling stations, and carports.

I saw Robert twice a week for 2 weeks before I introduced a new aspect into our sessions. I began to use some relaxation training with Robert. He sat in a large armchair and followed my suggestions to relax his body. I then paired a pleasant image that he chose (playing happily with his truck) and an image of the toilet. Robert was asked to give me a number from 1 to 10 (1 meaning that he feels comfortable and 10 meaning that he feels upset) as he imaged these stimuli. Gradually Robert could image a toilet and say "One." When I was sure he could do this, I began a multitherapeutic approach with Robert, involving his parents as well. The plan involved the following:

1. *Bibliotherapy* – Robert's parents took turns reading a book to him from a selected list I gave them. These were stories about

characters who initially feared something but who conquered their fears. Fears were of the dark, of imaginary monsters, of moving, of going to school, and so on. I also made up stories called *Robert the Brave*. Each simple plot depicted Robert rescuing a small animal or going on a journey to a "scary" place, only to discover that the inhabitants were friendly people and animals. Robert was encouraged to draw any character or object he wished at the conclusion of each story. Robert also drew a "badge of courage" for himself, cut it out, and mounted it on cardboard.

2. *Arts and crafts* – Robert revealed to me that three things lived in the toilet that scared him – a snake, a crocodile, and a scary fish. "I know they are in my imagination, but I can't help it." Robert drew these animals over and over. He drew "spears and slingshots" to kill them and cages around them. Sometimes he crumpled the drawings, tore them up, and threw them in the wastebasket. He did this with glee, exorcising his frightening images. Robert also was encouraged to use Play Doh to make his animals and fish. He did this and squashed the forms when finished.

3. *Play therapy* – Not only did we continue our car and truck game, so that Robert would have some sense of fun and relief in our sessions, but I now introduced the toy toilet and miniature dolls from the doll house. Robert would put a Play Doh snake in the toilet and place the doll on the toilet. He verbalized his fears at first, but gradually he removed the "snake," saying, "It's really not there." He drew a picture of a snake emerging from a toilet. The snake "bit the boy on the face." He drew this several times during our sessions, until finally he stated, "This can't happen, because there really are no snakes in there." But Robert still needed paper over the hole in his parents' toilet.

4. *Visits to the zoo* – I encouraged the Frasers to take Robert to the local zoo to see the snakes and crocodiles, and to visit the aquarium to see the sharks. Fortunately, therapy carried over into the summer and overlapped with Mr. Fraser's vacation. The parents cooperated and visited these places.

5. *Behavior chart* – In my sessions with the Frasers, I discovered that Robert had no responsibilities at home. We set up a plan whereby Robert would perform two daily chores – take out the garbage and make his bed. He would get a star on a chart each day he complied. A week's worth of stars led to a small allowance. I wanted Robert to feel responsible and grown-up and to develop a more positive image. Later, his parents used this chart to reward Robert for staying in bed throughout the night. He used to come into their bed at 3 or 4 a.m., and that habit was annoying to them. Robert was learning how to become more self-reliant, and slowly he was overcoming not only the toilet phobia but also a fear of sleeping alone.

6. *Systematic densensitization and behavior modification* – I employed these techniques as my main forms of therapy while continuing to use these approaches. Very simply, I began to shape Robert's behavior by moving from my playroom to the hall, to the bathroom, to the toilet, to the handle, to watching me flush the toilet, to both of us flushing the toilet together, Robert flushing it alone, and entering the toilet alone. At each step, Robert reported a number to me. When he eventually could say "One," we proceeded to the next step. In addition, I offered Robert some images to protect him. He chose a "shield," a "light," and "Bigfoot." Armed with these protectors, he could approach his imaginary demons and remain in control of his fears. We did this over a 3-month period. At the same time, I demonstrated the technique to his parents, urging them to utilize it by starting with a second bathroom in their home and then generalizing to the grandparents' home, where Robert would feel safe and trusting.

Thus, with all of these approaches working simultaneously, progress was made. Robert was able to use both of his parents' bathrooms, followed by use of the bathrooms in the homes of both sets of grandparents. Soon he was able to use all four bathrooms, eliminating the need for paper over the holes. The drawings continued, but now Robert told me that he was no longer afraid of snakes and scary fish. He only drew crocodiles and molded them out of Play Doh. As these fears subsided, the Frasers took Robert and his brother on an all-day outing in a boat. I prepared Robert for this by discussing the toilet on the boat; that he could use paper if he really had to cover that hole; that he could use his protectors to help him; and by giving him ample time to draw his crocodiles and practice the relaxation technique.

Robert had a successful boat trip. He bounded into my playroom the next session to report that "I didn't even need paper on the hole." He was proud of himself. Robert began to see that he could try out strange bathrooms and remain safe. The exciting moment came when he announced that he was willing to go to my toilet alone when he had to urinate. He ran in by himself, urinated, and flushed the toilet. He came out grinning from ear to ear. This was the first time he had used a toilet by himself since the onset of the phobia. At home, at his grandparents' houses, and on the boat, a parent needed to be in the toilet with Robert. But now we had achieved a breakthrough in therapy, and soon it would generalize to his home and his grandparents' homes.

One important place needed to be confronted – the toilet in Robert's school. He would be entering first grade. This meant that there would no longer be a toilet in the classroom; he would have to go down the hall to a larger room. Robert would be in school all day and could not rely on a noontime rush home to urinate. I decided to use in vivo treatment, that is, treating Robert in the natural setting, the school. There have been reports in the literature of cases in which school phobias were successfully treated through a gradual step-by-step procedure, using a fear hierarchy from sitting on the steps of the school, to eventually moving indoors to the hall, to the classroom, to spending increasing amounts of time in the classroom, ranging from 10 minutes to the 7-hour school day (Houlihan & Jones, 1989). Because Robert had been successful with bathrooms at home, at his grandparents' homes, on the boat, and near my playroom, I felt he would progress more quickly than he would have if he had not had these previous positive experiences.

Summer had arrived (I had been treating Robert since April), school was closed, and this was an excellent time to carry out in vivo treatment. No other children would be present who might cause Robert embarrassment. I began working with Robert at his school during July and at the beginning of August for only five sessions. I followed the step-by-step procedure that I had used earlier in his treatment. We approached the bathroom that Robert would be using in the school while Robert used our number system and his protective images, which afforded him a sense of control. Robert was able to explore the bathrooms, enter the stalls with me, and watch me flush the two toilets and the three urinals. After this session, we talked about his feelings. Robert insisted that he did not need to draw his scary crocodiles and had no fear of "anything" in the toilet. He preferred to draw boats and flags instead.

After three sessions, which were similar in behavior modification technique, Robert was able to flush all the toilets and remain in the bathroom alone while I waited just outside the door, where he could hear me. Our sessions occurred in the morning after his breakfast. I suggested to his mother that Robert try to avoid urination until we met at school. As a result, at our fourth session, Robert announced that he needed to urinate. He was able to do so, preferring to use a stall rather than a urinal. He insisted that I remain outside the stall door. Robert closed the door, used no paper to cover the hole, urinated, and flushed the toilet. He emerged triumphant, beaming, and said, "I did it." He was clearly proud of this major accomplishment – and so was I.

I decided to try the same tactic the following week, reminding his mother that Robert should delay urination until our session. Robert came to school, eager to try using the bathroom alone. This time, he did so while I waited *outside* the bathroom door. Robert again felt joy and relief that he was able to remain in the bathroom alone while urinating. Robert and I summed up our experiences over the past few months at the end of this session. He had mastered his problem.

During our last session in the playroom, Robert asked if he

could tear up the remainder of his former drawings of the snakes, crocodiles, and scary fish. The phobia was no longer present, and in general, Robert had a more positive self-concept and felt more confident. He was able to remain in his own bed for the entire night, continued to do his chores around the house, and as he put it, "I know what 'responsible' means."

The maturity that Robert had gained over the months of therapy helped him to gain control over the toilet phobia that had been crippling him for so long. I am optimistic that Robert will maintain his accomplishment and that it will generalize to other bathroom situations.

Summary

I began this chapter with the premise that play can be healing. As Levenson and Herman (1991, p. 660) state, "the relationship between therapist and the child is crucial in order to set the stage for the intervention to have a successful outcome." They call that relationship a *working alliance*. I believe that the success in both Lois's and Robert's situations was attained because I tried to establish a supportive, nonjudgmental atmosphere. As the children began to trust me, they expressed their fears and anxieties. What they could not put into words emerged through their play or artwork. Our alliance, based on trust and mutual respect, led to important changes in each child. Lois was better able to endure the pain of loss, and Robert began to master a paralyzing phobia. Images of terrible consequences that had led to the pain of both of these children became a source of strength as they played out their fantasies and recovered.

References

Almqvist, B. (1989a). Age and gender differences in children's Christmas requests. *Play and Culture, 2,* 2–19.

Almqvist, B. (1989b). Children and toys: A bibliography. Uppsala Reports on Education, No. 27. Uppsala, Sweden.

Andreas, C. (1969). War toys and the peace movement. *Journal of Social Issues, 25,* 83–99.

Axelrod, R., & Hamilton, W. D. (1981). The evolution of cooperation. *Science, 211,* 1390–1396.

Barker, R. G. (1968). *Ecological psychology.* Stanford, CA: Stanford University Press.

Barker, R. G., & Wright, H. F. (1955). *One boy's day.* New York: Harpers.

Baron, R. A. (1977). *Human aggression.* New York: Plenum.

Bateson, G. (1972). *Steps to an ecology of mind.* New York: Ballantine.

Bell, N. J., & Carver, W. (1980). A re-evaluation of gender label effects: Expectant mothers' responses to infants. *Child Development, 51,* 927.

Berenbaum, S. A., & Hines, M. (1992). Early androgens are related to childhood sex-typed toy preferences. *Psychological Science, 3,* 203–206.

Beresin, A. R. (1989). Toy war games and the illusion of two-sided rhetoric. *Play and Culture, 2,* 218–224.

Berkowitz, L. (1984). Some effects of thought on anti- and prosocial influences of media events: A cognitive–neo-associationist analysis. *Psychological Bulletin, 95,* 410–427.

Berndt, T. J., & Heller, K. A. (1986). Gender stereotypes and social influence: A developmental study. *Journal of Personality and Social Psychology, 50,* 889–898.

Bettelheim, B. (1987, March). The importance of play. *The Atlantic.*

Bjorkqvist, K., Lagerspetz, K. M. J., & Kaukiainen, K. (1991). The development of direct and indirect strategies: Gender differences during ages 8, 11, 15, and 18. *Aggressive Behavior, 17*, 60.

Bjorkqvist, K., & Niemela, P. (1992). *Of mice and women: Aspects of female aggression*. San Diego, CA: Academic Press.

Blumer, H. (1973). Der methodologische Standort des Symbolischen Interaktionismus. *Arbeitsgruppe Bielefelder Soziologen: Alltagswissen, Interaktion und gesellschaftliche Wirklichkeit* [The methodological position of symbolic interaction. *Knowledge of everyday life, interaction and social reality*], *1*, 189–210.

Bonnafont, G. (1992, October). *Video games and the child*. Paper presented at a seminar on Myths and Realities of Play. London.

Bonnafont, G. (no date). *Jeu video et résultats scolaires*. Dijon: Centre d'Etudes et de Communication.

Boyanowsky, E. O., Newtson, D., & Walster, E. (1974). Film preferences following a murder. *Communication Research, 1*, 32–43.

British Toy and Hobby Association. (1990). *Aggressive toys: A guide for concerned parents*. London: Author.

Bronfenbrenner, U. (1979). *The ecology of human development*. Cambridge, MA: Harvard University Press.

Brougère, G. (1985). La place du jeu et du matériel ludique à l'école maternelle. [The disposal of toys and play materials in l'école maternelle.] Laboratoire de Recherche sur le Jeu et le Jouet. Paris: Université Paris-Nord.

Brown, R. M., Brown, N. L., & Reid, K. (1992). Evidence for a player's position advantage in a videogame. *Perceptual and Motor Skills, 74*, 547–554.

Bruner, J. S. (1986). *Actual minds, possible worlds*. Cambridge, MA: Harvard University Press.

Bunker, L. K. (1991). The role of play and motor skill development in building children's self-confidence and self-esteem. *Elementary School Journal, 91*, 467–471.

Caldera, Y., Huston, A., & O'Brien, M. (1989). Social interactions and actions and play patterns of parents and toddlers with feminine, masculine and neutral toys. *Child Development, 60*, 70–76.

Carlsson-Paige, N., & Levin, D. E. (1987). *The war play dilemma: Balancing needs and values in the early childhood classroom*. New York: Teachers College Press.

Carlsson-Paige, N., & Levin, D. E. (1990). *Who's calling the shots? How to respond effectively to children's fascination with war play and war toys*. Philadelphia: New Society.

Carvalho, A. M. A., Smith, P. K., Hunter, T., & Costabile, A. (1990). Playground activities for boys and girls: Developmental and cultural trends in children's perceptions of gender differences. *Play and Culture, 3,* 343–347.

Casey, R. J., & Berman, J. S. (1985). The outcome of psychotherapy with children. *Psychological Bulletin, 98,* 388–400.

Catherall, T. S. (1989). Playing with electric trains in school classrooms. *Play and Culture, 2,* 137–141.

Chaillé, C. (1978). The child's conceptions of play, pretending, and toys: Sequences and structural parallels. *Human Development, 21,* 201–210.

Charlesworth, W. (1988). Resources and resource acquisition during ontogeny. In K. MacDonald (Ed.), *Sociobiological perspectives on human development.* New York: Springer-Verlag.

Connolly, J., Doyle, A. B., & Reznick, E. (1988). Social pretend play and social interaction in preschoolers. *Journal of Applied Developmental Psychology, 9,* 301–313.

Connor, K. (1989). Aggression: Is it in the eye of the beholder? *Play and Culture, 2,* 213–217.

Cook-Gumperz, J. (1977). Situated instructions. In S. Ervin-Tripp & C. Mitchell-Kernan (Eds.), *Child discourse.* New York: Academic Press.

Cooper, J., Hall, J., & Huff, C. (1990). Situational stress as a consequence of sex-stereotyped software. *Personality and Social Psychology Bulletin, 16,* 419–429.

Costabile, A., Genta, M. L., Zucchini, E., Smith, P. K., & Harker, R. (1992). Attitudes of parents to war play in young children. *Early Education and Development, 3,* 356–369.

Costabile, A., Smith, P. K., Matheson, L., Aston, J., Hunter, T., & Boulton, M. (1991). Cross-national comparison of how children distinguish serious and playful fighting. *Developmental Psychology, 27,* 881–887.

Creasey, G., & Myers, B. (1986). Video games and children: Effects on leisure activities, schoolwork, and peer involvement. *Merrill-Palmer Quarterly, 32*(3), 251–261.

Csikszentmihalyi, M. (1976). What play says about behavior. *Ontario Psychologist, 8*(2), 5–11.

Darwin, C. (1872/1965). *The expression of emotions in animals and man.* Chicago: University of Chicago Press.

Dennett, D. (1991). *Consciousness explained.* Boston: Little, Brown.

de Waal, F. (1986). The integration of dominance and social bonding in primates. *Quarterly Review of Biology, 61,* 459–479.

DiPietro, J. A. (1981). Rough and tumble play: A function of gender. *Developmental Psychology, 17,* 50–58.

Dunn, J. (1988). *The beginnings of social understanding.* Cambridge, MA: Harvard University Press.

Eaton, W. O., & Enns, L. R. (1986). Sex differences in human motor activity level. *Psychological Bulletin, 100,* 19–28.

Eckerman, C. O., & Stein, M. R. (1990). How imitation begets imitation and toddlers' generation of games. *Developmental Psychology, 26,* 370–378.

Eisen, G. (1988). *Children and play in the Holocaust.* Amherst: University of Massachusetts Press.

Eisenberg, N., Tryon, K., & Cameron, E. (1984). The relation of pre-schoolers' peer interaction to their sex-typed toy choices. *Child Development, 55,* 1044–1050.

Eisenberg, N., Wolchik, S. A., Hernandez, R., & Pasternack, J. F. (1985). Parental socialization of young children's play. *Child Development, 56,* 1506–1513.

Elias, N. (1982). *The civilizing process.* New York: Pantheon.

Erikson, E. H. (1977). *Toys and reasons.* New York: Norton.

Esman, A. H. (1983). Psychoanalytic play therapy. In C. E. Schaefer & K. J. O'Connor (Eds.), *Handbook of play therapy.* New York: Wiley.

Fagot, B. I. (1974). Sex differences in toddlers' behaviour and parental reaction. *Developmental Psychology, 10,* 554–558.

Fagot, B. I. (1984). Teacher and peer reactions to boys' and girls' play styles. *Sex Roles, 11,* 691–702.

Fein, G. (1981a). Pretend play: Creativity and consciousness. In D. Gorlitz & J. Wöhwill (Eds.), *Curiosity, imagination, and play.* Hillsdale, NJ: Erlbaum.

Fein, G. (1981b). Pretend play: An integrative review. *Child Development, 52,* 1095–1118.

Fein, G., Johnson, D., Kosson, N., Stork, L., & Wasserman, L. (1975). Sex stereotypes and preferences in the toy choices of 20-month-old boys and girls. *Developmental Psychology, 11,* 527–528.

Flavell, J. H. (1991). What young children know about the mind. *Contemporary Psychology, 36,* 741–742.

Flavell, J. H., Flavell, E. R., & Green, F. L. (1987). Young children's knowledge about the apparent–real and pretend–real distinctions. *Developmental Psychology, 23,* 816–822.

Foucault, M. (1973). *Madness and civilization.* New York: Vintage.

Frazer, J. G. (1949). *The golden bough.* London: Macmillan.

Freedman, J. L. (1986). Television violence and aggression: A rejoinder. *Psychological Bulletin, 100,* 372–378.

Freud, S. (1920/1962). *Beyond the pleasure principle.* In *Standard Edition of the Collected Psychological Works,* Vol. 18. London: Hogarth.

Friedrich-Cofer, L., & Huston, A. C. (1986). Television violence and aggression: The debate continues. *Psychological Bulletin, 100,* 364–371.

Fry, D. P. (1990). Play aggression among Zapotec children: Implications for the practice hypothesis. *Aggressive Behavior, 16,* 321–340.

Funk, J. B. (1992). Video games: Benign or malignant? *Developmental and Behavioral Pediatrics, 13,* 53–54.

Garvey, C. (1991). *Play* (2nd ed.). Cambridge, MA: Harvard University Press.

Garvey, C. (in press). Inter-subjectivity and framing in pretend play interactions. *Human Development.*

Giddings, M., & Halverson, C. F. (1981). Young children's use of toys in home environments. *Family Relations, 30*(1), 69–74.

Glickman, C. (1981). Play and the school curriculum: The historical context. *Journal of Research and Development in Education, 14*(3), 1–10.

Goldstein, J. H. (1983). *Sports violence.* New York: Springer-Verlag.

Goldstein, J. H. (1988). *Children and aggressive toys.* London: British Toy and Hobby Association.

Goldstein, J. H. (1992a). *"War toys": A review of empirical research.* London: British Toy and Hobby Association.

Goldstein, J. H. (1992b). Sex differences in aggressive play and toy preference. In K. Bjorkqvist & P. Niemela (Eds.), *Of mice and women: Aspects of female aggression.* San Diego, CA: Academic Press.

Greenfield, P. M. (1984). *Mind and media: The effects of television, video games and computers.* Cambridge, MA: Harvard University Press.

Greenwell, J. (1988, November 29). Shooting times. *The Guardian.*

Greer, D., Potts, P., Wright, J. C., & Huston, A. C. (1982). The effects of television commercial form and commercial placement on children's social behaviour and attention. *Child Development, 53,* 611–619.

Gump, P. (1989). Ecological psychology and issues of play. In M. Bloch & A. D. Pellegrini (Eds.), *The ecological contexts of children's Play.* Norwood, NJ: Ablex.

Haft, H. (1984). Inhaltsanalyse [Content analysis]. In H. Haft & K. Kordes (Eds.), *Enzyklopaedia Erziehungswissenschaft: Vol. 2, Methoden der Erziehungs- und Bildungsforschung.* Stuttgart.

Halliday, M. (1969/1970). Relevant models of language. *Educational Review, 22,* 26–37.

Harris, P. (1990). The child's theory of mind and its cultural context. In G. Butterworth & P. Bryant (Eds.), *Causes of development.* New York: Harvester Wheatsheaf.

Hastorf, A. H., & Cantril, H. (1954). They saw a game: A case study. *Journal of Abnormal and Social Psychology, 47,* 574–576.

Hattiangadi, J. N. (1987). *How is language possible?* La Salle, IN: Open Court Press.

Heath, S. B. (1983). *Ways with words.* New York: Cambridge University Press.

Heinze, T. (1987). *Qualitative Sozialforschung [Qualitative Social Research]*. Opladen, Germany.

Hinde, R. A. (1976). On describing relationships. *Journal of Child Psychology and Psychiatry, 17,* 1–19.

Houlihan, D. D., & Jones, R. N. (1989). Treatment of a boy's phobia with in vivo systematic desensitization. *Professional School Psychology, 4*(4), 285–293.

Huizinga, J. (1956). *Homo Ludens. Vom Ursprung der Kultur im Spiel [Homo Ludens: On the Origins of Culture in Play]*. Hamburg.

Humphreys, A., & Smith, P. K. (1987). Rough-and-tumble in preschool and playground. In P. K. Smith (Ed.), *Play in animals and humans.* London: Basil Blackwell.

Huston, A. (1983). Sex-typing. In E. M. Hetherington (Ed.), *Handbook of child psychology.* Vol. 4. New York: Wiley.

Hymes, D. (1971). Competence and performance in linguistic theory. In R. Huxley & E. Ingram (Eds.), *Language acquisition: Models and methods.* New York: Academic Press.

Izard, C. (1991). *The psychology of emotions.* New York: Plenum.

Jacobs, G. (1992). Hypermedia and discovery-based learning: A historical perspective. *British Journal of Educational Technology, 23,* 113–121.

James, W. (1890/1952). *The principles of psychology.* New York: Dover.

Jukes, J. (1991). *Children and aggressive toys: Empirical studies of toy preference.* Unpublished doctoral dissertation, University College, London.

Jukes, J., & Goldstein, J. H. (1993). Preference for aggressive toys. *International Play Journal, 1,* 81–91.

Karpoe, K., & Olney, R. (1983). The effect of boys' or girls' toys on sex-typed play in preadolescents. *Sex Roles, 9,* 507–518.

Kestenbaum, G. I., & Weinstein, L. (1985). Personality, psychopathology, and developmental issues in male adolescent game use. *Journal of the American Academy of Child Psychiatry, 24,* 329–337.

Kinder, M. (1991). *Playing with power in movies, television, and video games.* Berkeley: University of California Press.

King, C. E. (1978). *Encyclopedia of toys.* London: Quarto.

Kline, S., & Pentecost, D. (1990). The characterization of play: Marketing children's toys. *Play and Culture, 3,* 235–255.

Köckeis-Stangl, E. (1984). Methoden der Sozialisationsforschung. In K. Hurrelmann & D. Ulich (Eds.), *Handbuch der Sozialisationsforschung.* Weinheim.

Kubey, R., & Larson, R. (1990). The use and experience of the new video media among children and young adolescents. *Communication Research, 17,* 107–130.

Langley, T., O'Neal, E. C., Craig, K. M., & Yost, E. A. (1992). Aggression-consistent, -inconsistent, and -irrelevant priming effects on selective exposure to media violence. *Aggressive Behavior, 18,* 349–356.

Leslie, A. M. (1987). Pretense and representation: The origins of "theory of mind." *Psychological Review, 94,* 412–422.

Levenson, R. L., Jr., & Herman, J. (1991). The use of role playing as a technique in the psychotherapy of children. *Psychotherapy, 28,* 660–665.

Lever, J. (1978). Sex differences in the complexity of children's play and games. *American Sociological Review, 43,* 471–483.

Lewin, K. (1954). Behavior and development as a function of the total situation. In L. Carmichael (Ed.), *Manual of child psychology.* New York: Wiley.

Lin, S., & Lepper, M. R. (1987). Correlates of children's usage of videogames and computers. *Journal of Applied Social Psychology, 17,* 72–93.

Little, M. (1989). *How far does the experimental evidence go in backing the claim that war toys and war play promotes "real" violence and aggression in children?* Unpublished B.A. dissertation, University of Sheffield, England.

Lovaas, O. I. (1961). Effect of exposure to symbolic aggression on aggressive behavior. *Child Development, 32,* 37–44.

Maccoby, E. E., & Jacklin, C. N. (1974). *The psychology of sex differences.* Stanford, CA: Stanford University Press.

Malone, T. W. (1981). Toward a theory of intrinsically motivating instruction. *Cognitive Science, 5,* 333–370.

Mandler, G. (1984). *Mind and body: Psychology of emotion and stress.* New York: Norton.

McCrae, R. R., & John, O. P. (1992). An introduction to the five factor model and its applications. *Journal of Personality, 60*(2), 175–216.

McLoyd, V. (1982). Social class differences in sociodramatic play: A critical review. *Developmental Review, 2,* 1–30.

McLoyd, V. (1983). The effects of the structure of play objects on the pretend play of low-income children. *Child Development, 54,* 626–635.

McLoyd, V. (1986). Scaffolds or shackles? The role of toys in preschool children's pretend play. In G. Fein & M. Rivkin (Eds.), *The young child at play: Reviews of research,* Vol. 4. Washington, DC: National Association for the Education of Young Children.

Meyer-Bahlburg, H. F. L., Feldman, J. F., Cohen, P., & Ehrhardt, A. A. (1988). Perinatal factors in the development of gender-related play behavior: Sex hormones versus pregnancy complications. *Psychiatry, 51,* 260–271.

Miedzian, M. (1991). *Boys will be boys: Breaking the link between masculinity and violence.* New York: Doubleday.

Moller, L. C., Hymel, S., & Rubin, K. H. (1992). Sex typing in play and popularity in middle childhood. *Sex Roles, 26,* 331–353.

Mummendey, A. (1983). Aggressive Verhalten [Aggressive behavior]. In H. Thormae (Ed.), *Enzyklopaedie der Psychologie.* Göttingen.

Nagel, T. (1974). What is it like to be a bat? *Philosophical Review, 83,* 435–450.

Nakamine, A. (1979). Yooji no schoochooasobi ni oyobosu ganguto-kuesei no kooka [Effects of toy type on children's imaginative play]. *Japanese Journal of Educational Psychology, 27,* 62–66.

Ng, D. (1990, June). *Exciting play: Arcade video gaming and youth.* Paper presented at the annual meeting of the International Association for the Child's Right to Play, Tokyo.

O'Brien, M., & Huston, A. (1985). Development of sex-typed behavior in toddlers. *Developmental Psychology, 21,* 866–871.

O'Connor, K. J. (1991). *The play therapy primer.* New York: Wiley.

Orr, R., Jr. (1976). T is for teddybear: Teddy can read. *Language Arts, 53,* 883–885.

Parker, S. T. (1984). Playing for keeps: An evolutionary perspective on human games. In P. K. Smith (Ed.), *Play in animals and humans.* Oxford: Basil Blackwell.

Parten, M. (1933). Social play among preschool children. *Journal of Abnormal and Social Psychology, 28,* 136–147.

Patterson, G. R., DeBaryshe, B. D., & Ramsey, E. (1989). A developmental perspective on antisocial behavior. *American Psychologist, 44,* 329–335.

Pellegrini, A. D. (1982). The generation of cohesive text by preschoolers in two play contexts. *Discourse Processes, 5,* 101–108.

Pellegrini, A. D. (1983). Sociolinguistic contexts of the preschool. *Journal of Applied Developmental Psychology, 4,* 397–405.

Pellegrini, A. D. (1984). The social cognitive ecology of the preschool classroom. *International Journal of Behavioral Development, 7,* 321–332.

Pellegrini, A. D. (1985). The narrative organization of children's fantasy play: The effects of age and play context. *Educational Psychology, 5,* 17–25.

Pellegrini, A. D. (1986). Play centers and the production of imaginative language. *Discourse Processes, 9,* 115–125.

Pellegrini, A. D. (1987a). The effect of play context on the development of children's verbalized fantasy. *Semiotica, 65,* 285–293.

Pellegrini, A. D. (1987b). Rough-and-tumble play: Developmental and educational significance. *Educational Psychologist, 22,* 23–43.

Pellegrini, A. D. (1988). Elementary-school children's rough-and-tumble play and social competence. *Developmental Psychology, 24,* 802–806.

Pellegrini, A. D., & Perlmutter, J. (1988). The role of verbal conflicts in preschool children's social-cognitive development. In A. D. Pellegrini (Ed.), *Psychological bases for early education*. Chichester, U.K.: Wiley.

Pellegrini, A. D., & Perlmutter, J. (1989). Classroom contextual effects on children's play. *Developmental Psychology, 25,* 289–296.

Perlmutter, J., & Pellegrini, A. D. (1987). Children's verbalized fantasy with parents and peers. *Educational Psychology, 7,* 269–281.

Piaget, J. (1962). *Play, dreams and imitation in childhood.* New York: Norton.

Piaget, J. (1965). *The moral development of the child.* New York: Free Press.

Piaget, J. (1983). Piaget's theory. In W. Kessen (Ed.), *Handbook of child psychology.* Vol. 1. New York: Wiley.

Provenzo, E. F., Jr. (1991). *Video kids: Making sense of Nintendo.* Cambridge, MA: Harvard University Press.

Pulaski, M. A. (1973). Toys and imaginative play. In J. L. Singer (Ed.), *The child's world of make-believe.* New York: Academic Press.

Pulaski, M. A. (1970). Play as a function of toy structure and fantasy predisposition. *Child Development, 41,* 530–537.

Quilitch, R. H. (1974). *How educational are educational toys?* Washington, DC: Dept. of Health, Education, and Welfare.

Quilitch, R. H., & Risley, T. (1973). The effects of play materials on social play. *Journal of Applied Behavior Analysis, 6,* 573–578.

Repetti, R. L. (1984). Determinants of children's sex stereotyping: Parental sex-role traits and television viewing. *Personality and Social Psychology Bulletin, 10,* 457–468.

Rheingold, H., & Cook, K. V. (1975). The contents of boys' and girls' rooms as an index of parents' behavior. *Child Development, 46,* 459–463.

Richardson, J. G., & Simpson, C. G. (1982). Children, gender, and social structure: An analysis of the contents of letters to Santa Claus. *Child Development, 53,* 429–436.

Robinson, C., & Jackson, R. (1987). The effects of varying toy detail within a prototypical play object on the solitary pretend play of preschool children. *Journal of Applied Developmental Psychology, 8,* 209–220.

Roeder, B., & Masendorf, F. (1979). Differentielle Wirksamkeit von spielerischen vers ubenden Lernmaterialien bei leistungsschwachen Kindern in zweiten Schuljahr [Differential effects of aid materials and learning toys on pupils with achievement deficiencies during their second school year]. *Psychologie in Erziehung und Unterricht, 26*(1), 22–26.

Roopnarine, J. L., Ahmeduzzaman, M., Hossain, Z., & Reigraf, N. B. (1992). Parent–infant rough play: Its cultural specificity. *Early Education and Development, 3,* 298–311.

Rosenfeld, E. F. (1975), *The relationship of sex-typed toys to the development of competency and sex-role identification*. Paper presented to the Society for Research in Child Development, Denver.

Ross, H., & Taylor, H. (1989). Do boys prefer daddy or his physical style of play? *Sex Roles, 20*, 23–33.

Rubin, K. H., Fein, G. G., & Vandenberg, B. (1983). Play. In P. H. Mussen (Ed.), *Manual of child psychology*. Vol. 4. New York: Wiley.

Ruble, D., Balaban, T., & Cooper, J. (1981). Gender constancy and the effects of sex-typed televised toy commercials. *Child Development, 52*, 667–673.

Sachs, J., Goldman, J., & Chaillé, C. (1984). Planning in pretend play. In A. D. Pellegrini & T. Yawkey (Eds.), *The development of oral and written language in social contexts*. Norwood, NJ: Ablex.

Saturday Review/World. (1974). Can toys really teach? Vol. *11*(16), 60–62.

Schachtel, E. G. (1959). *Metamorphosis: On the development of affect, perception, attention and memory*. New York: Basic Books.

Schmitt, B. D. (1992, February). Is your child overdosing on video games? *Contemporary Pediatrics*, 105–106.

Schwartz, L. A., & Markham, W. T. (1985). Sex stereotyping in children's toy advertisements. *Sex Roles, 12*, 157–170.

Serbin, L. A., Conner, J. M., Burchardt, C. J., Citron, C.D. (1979). Effects of peer pressure on sex-typing of children's play behavior. *Journal of Experimental Child Psychology, 27*, 303–309.

Shell, R., & Eisenberg, N. (1990). The role of peers' gender in children's naturally occurring interest in toys. *International Journal of Behavioral Development, 13*, 373–388.

Shmukler, D. (1981). Mother–child interaction and its relationship to the predisposition to imaginative play. *Genetic Psychology Monographs, 104*, 215–235.

Singer, D. G. (1993). *Playing for their lives: How troubled children are helped by play therapy*. New York: Free Press.

Singer, D. G., & Singer, J. L. (1990). *The house of make-believe: Play and the developing imagination*. Cambridge, MA: Harvard University Press.

Singer, J. L. (1974). *Imagery and daydream methods in psychotherapy and behavior modification*. New York: Academic Press.

Singer, J. L., & Singer, D. G. (1981). *Television, imagination and aggression: A study of preschoolers*. Hillsdale, NJ: Erlbaum.

Smilansky, S. (1968). *Effects of sociodramatic play on disadvantaged preschool children*. New York: Wiley.

Smith, M. L., Glass, G. V., & Miller, T. I. (1980). *Psychotherapy*. Baltimore: Johns Hopkins University Press.

Smith, P. K. (1982). How important is fantasy play? *Set: Research Information for Teachers*, No. 2.

Smith, P. K. (1983). Training in fantasy play. *Early Child Development and Care, 11*, 217–226.

Smith, P. K. (1988). Children's play and its role in early development: A re-evaluation of the "play ethos." In A. D. Pellegrini (Ed.), *Psychological bases for early education*. Chichester, U.K.: Wiley.

Smith, P. K. (1989). The role of rough-and-tumble play in the development of social competence: Theoretical perspectives and empirical evidence. In B. H. Schneider, G. Attili, J. Nadel, & R. P. Weissberg (Eds.), *Social competence in developmental perspective*. Dordrecht, the Netherlands: Kluwer.

Smith, P. K., & Bennett, S. (1990). Here come the steel monsters! *Changes, 8*(2), 97–105.

Smith, P. K., & Boulton, M. (1990). Rough-and-tumble play, aggression and dominance: Perception and behavior in children's encounters. *Human Development, 33*, 271–282.

Smith, P. K., Dalgliesh, M., & Herzmark, G. (1981). A comparison of the effects of fantasy play tutoring and skills tutoring in nursery classes. *International Journal of Behavioral Development, 4*, 421–441.

Smith, P. K., Hunter, T., Carvalho, A. M. A., & Costabile, A. (1992). Children's perceptions of playfighting, play-chasing and real fighting: A cross-national interview study. *Social Development, 1*, 211–229.

Sneed, C., & Runco, M. A. (1992). The beliefs adults and children hold about television and video games. *Journal of Psychology, 126*, 273–284.

Suito, N., & Reifel, S. (1992, May). *Gender differences in Japanese and American sociodramatic play*. Paper presented to the International Council for Child's Play, Paris.

Sutton-Smith, B. (1968). Novel responses to toys. *Merrill-Palmer Quarterly, 14*(2), 151–158.

Sutton-Smith, B. (1983). Die Idealisierung des Spiels [The idealization of play]. In O. Grupe (Ed.), *Spiel-Spiele-Spielen* [Play-games-playing]. Schorndorf.

Sutton-Smith, B. (1986). *Toys as culture*. New York: Gardner Press.

Sutton-Smith, B. (1988). War toys and childhood aggression. *Play and Culture, 1*, 57–69.

Sutton-Smith, B. (1992). Commentary: At play in the public arena. *Early Education and Development, 3*, 390–400.

Sutton-Smith, B. (in press). Paradigms of play. In J. Hellendorn, R. van der Kooij, & B. Sutton-Smith (Eds.), *Play and intervention*. Albany, NY: SUNY Press.

Sutton-Smith, B., Gerstmyer, J., & Meckley, A. (1988). Play-fighting as folkplay amongst preschool children. *Western Folklore, 47*, 161–176.

Sutton-Smith, B., & Kelly-Byrne, D. (1984). The idealization of play. In P. K. Smith (Ed.), *Play in animals and humans*. London: Basil Blackwell.

Sutton-Smith, B., & Magee, M. A. (1989). Reversible childhood. *Play and Culture, 2*, 52–63.

Taylor, M. (1992, August). *The role of emotion in children's ability to distinguish fantasy from reality*. Paper presented at the meeting of the American Psychological Association, Washington, DC.

Tomkins, S. S. (1962). *Affect, imagery, consciousness*. New York: Springer.

Tomkins, S. S. (1970). A theory of memory. In J. S. Antrobus (Ed.), *Cognition and affect*. Boston: Little, Brown.

Tracy, D. M. (1987). Toys, spatial ability, and science and mathematics achievement: Are they related? *Sex Roles, 17*, 251–260.

Trivers, R. (1971). The evolution of reciprocal altruism. *Quarterly Review of Biology, 46*, 35–57.

Tuchscherer, P. (1988). *TV interactive toys: The new high tech threat to children*. Bend, OR: Pinnaroo.

Tudge, J., & Rogoff, B. (1989). Peer influences on cognitive development: Piagetian and Vygotskian perspectives. In M. Bornstein & J. Bruner (Eds.), *Interaction in human development*. Hillsdale, NJ: Erlbaum.

Twitchell, J. (1989). *Preposterous violence*. Oxford: Oxford University Press.

Vagt, G., & Müller, E. (1976). Erfolgskontrolle eines Lernspielzeugs [A follow-up control of some educational toys]. *Zeitschrift fur Entwicklungspsychologie und Padagogische Psychologie, 8* (1), 44–50.

Vandenberg, B. (1987). *Toys and intentions*. Paper presented at the meeting of the International Council on Children's Play, Suhl, Germany.

Vandivert, W., & Vandivert, R. (1974). Past teaching aids in jigsaw puzzles. *Smithsonian, 5*(5).

Velmans, M. (1990). Consciousness, brain and the physical world. *Philosophical Psychology, 3*, 77–99.

Vieira, K. G., & Miller, W. H. (1978). Avoidance of sex-atypical toys by five- and ten-year-old children. *Psychological Reports, 43*, 543–546.

Vygotsky, L. (1962). *Thought and language*. Cambridge, MA: MIT Press.

Vygotsky, L. (1967). Play and its role in the mental development of the child. *Soviet Psychology, 12* (6), 62–76.

Vygotsky, L. (1978). *Mind in society*. Cambridge, MA: Harvard University Press.

Watson, M. W., & Peng, Y. (1992). The relation between toy gun play and children's aggressive behavior. *Early Education and Development, 3*, 370–389.

Wegener-Spöhring, G. (1985). Faszination am Kriegsspielzeug: Was ist zu tun? [Fascination with war toys: What has to be done?] *Grundschule, 17*(11), 46–49.

Wegener-Spöhring, G. (1986). Die Bedeutung von "Kriegsspielzeug" in der Lebenswelt von Grundschulkindern [The significance of "war toys" in the world of elementary school children]. *Zeitschrift fur Padagogik, 36,* 797–810.

Wegener-Spöhring, G. (1989a). War toys and aggressive games. *Play and Culture, 2,* 35–47.

Wegener-Spöhring, G. (1989b). Die balancierte Aggressivitat. Beobachtung und Interpretationen von Freispielszenen in Kindergarten [Balanced aggressiveness: The observation and interpretation of play periods in kindergartens]. *Spielmittel,* No. 2, 32–39.

Wegener-Spöhring, G. (1989c). Aggressive Spiele bei Kindern: Beobachtung und Interpretation von Freispielszenen [Aggressive games of children: Observation and interpretation of free play periods]. *Bildung und Erziehung, 42,* 103–120.

Weintraub, M., Clemens, L. P., Sockloff, A., Ethridge, T., Gracely, E., & Myers, B. (1984). The development of sex role stereotypes in the third year: Relationships to gender labelling, gender identity, sex-typed toy preference, and family characteristics. *Child Development, 55,* 1493–1503.

Wellman, H. M. (1990). *The child's theory of the mind.* Cambridge, MA: MIT Press.

Wilczak, P. (1976, December). The Teddy bear's picnic. *Instructor,* p. 69.

Willner, A. H. (1991). Behavioral deficiencies of aggressive 8–9-year-old boys: An observational study. *Aggressive Behavior, 17,* 135–154.

Wilson, T. P. (1973). Theorien der Interaktion und Modelle Soziologischer Erklärung. *Arbeitsgruppe Bielefelder Soziologen, 1,* 54–79.

Wolf, D., & Grollman, S. (1982). Ways of playing. In D. Pepler & K. Rubin (Eds.), *The play of children.* Basel: Karger.

Young, B. M. (1991). *Television advertising and children.* Oxford: Oxford University Press.

Zammuner, V. L. (1987). Children's sex-role stereotypes: A cross-cultural analysis. In P. Shaver & C. Hendrick (Eds.), *Review of personality and social psychology* (Vol. 7, Newbury Park). CA: Sage.

Zillmann, D. (1991). Television viewing and physiological arousal. In J. Bryant & D. Zillmann (Eds.), *Responding to the screen.* Hillsdale, NJ: Erlbaum.

Name Index

Subject Index